Managing People and Organisations

Edited by Stephen Taylor and Carol Woodhams

The only textbooks mapped to the CIPD Intermediate level learning outcomes:

Studying Human Resource Management, *Developing People and Organisations*, and *Managing People and Organisations*, together cover all of the learning outcomes for the core and optional units in Human Resource Management and Human Resource Development.

Series editors:

Stephen Taylor is a Senior Lecturer in Human Resource Management at the University of Exeter. He is also a Chief Examiner for the CIPD.

Carol Woodhams is a Senior Lecturer in Human Resource Management at the University of Exeter. She is CIPD National Examiner for Designing and Delivering Training.

Jim Stewart is Professor of HRD at Coventry University. He is also Chief Examiner of Learning and Development for the CIPD, as well as Visiting Panel Chair and External Moderator.

Studying Human Resource Management , **edited by Stephen Taylor and Carol Woodhams**

Contributors: Ted Johns, Graham Perkins, Krystal Wilkinson

Developing People and Organisations , **edited by Jim Stewart and Patricia Rogers**

Contributors: Jill Ashley-Jones, Susan Barnes, Terrence Wendell Brathwaite, Gary Connor, Amanda Lee, Rosalind Maxwell-Harrison, Michael McFadden, Sharon McGuire, Michelle McLardy, Ian McLean, Sophie Mills, Graham Perkins, Krish Pinto, Raymond Rogers, Dalbir Sidhu, Kirsten Stevens, Carol Woodhams

Managing People and Organisations , **edited by Stephen Taylor and Carol Woodhams**

Contributors: Cecilia Ellis, Ted Johns, Graham Perkins, Gail Swift, Krystal Wilkinson

The Chartered Institute of Personnel and Development is the leading publisher of books and reports for personnel and training professionals, students, and all those concerned with the effective management and development of people at work. For details of all our titles, please contact the publishing department:
tel: 020 8612 6204
e-mail: publishling@cipd.co.uk
The catalogue of all CIPD titles can be viewed on the CIPD website:
www.cipd.co.uk/bookstore

Managing People and Organisations

Edited by Stephen Taylor and Carol Woodhams

Chartered Institute of Personnel and Development

Published by the Chartered Institute of Personnel and Development,

151, The Broadway, London, SW19 1JQ

This edition first published 2012

Reprinted 2013, 2015

Styled by Exeter Premedia, India

Printed in Great Britain by Bell & Bain, Glasgow

British Library Cataloguing in Publication Data

A catalogue of this publication is available from the British Library

ISBN 978 1 84398 314 9

Chartered Institute of Personnel and Development,
151, The Broadway, London, SW19 1JQ
Tel: 020 8612 6200
E-mail: cipd@cipd.co.uk
Website: www.cipd.co.uk
Incorporated by Royal Charter.
Registered Charity No. 1079797

Contents

List of Figures and Tables

Contributor Biographies

Stephen Taylor is a Senior Lecturer in Human Resource Management at the University of Exeter Business School and also Chief Examiner for the Chartered Institute of Personnel and Development (CIPD). He previously taught at Manchester Business School, at Manchester Metropolitan University Business School, and worked in a variety of HR management roles in the hotel industry and in the NHS. He is the author/co-author of several books on HRM and employment law. He regularly represents parties in employment tribunals and undertakes HR consultancy and training work.

Dr Carol Woodhams is a Senior Lecturer in Human Resource Management at the University of Exeter Business School. She has held a number of positions within the CIPD, including National Examiner for Designing and Delivering Training, External Moderator for the Advanced Qualification, and editor of the flexible learning materials at Intermediate and Advanced levels. She previously taught at Plymouth University and Manchester Metropolitan University. Her specialist teaching subjects are employee resourcing and equality and diversity. Her research topics include studies of gender and disability discrimination in the UK and China. Prior to her academic career she held posts in management in the hospitality sector.

Cecilia Ellis is a Senior Lecturer in Human Resource Management at the Manchester Metropolitan University Business School. She teaches postgraduate and undergraduate students and is course leader for the MSc HRM and IHRM full-time programme. Cecilia holds Fellow membership of the Chartered Institute of Personnel and Development (FCIPD) and previously worked as a HR Business Partner for a multinational company.

Ted Johns has been – and continues as – a Chief Examiner first for the IPM, then the IPD and now the CIPD, for over 30 years. He was responsible for the adoption of the Big Idea of the Thinking Performer as the strategic vision for HR professionalism, and was recently delighted to be elected as a Companion Member of the Institute. He has written or co-authored books on ethical leadership, organisational change, customer care, world-class customer service excellence and time management. He is currently working on a book for the CIPD about employee engagement. Ted was a founder director of the Institute of Customer Service and officiated as its Chairman for seven years before retiring in 2009. He is a noted conference and seminar speaker not only in the UK but also in many other parts of the world.

Graham Perkins is a PhD student at Plymouth University. His PhD is focused on how idea generation can best be enabled within SMEs. Alongside his studies Graham works as an HR consultant for a variety of organisations and has a broad spectrum of experience from learning and development projects through to facilitating and analysing staff surveys.

Gail Swift is a senior Organisational Development (OD) and Learning Specialist with extensive experience in the public sector. She is currently a Deputy Director of OD in the NHS, responsible for strategic learning policy and governance and leadership and management development. She has previously held a variety of HR and management roles in the NHS and the private retail sector. She regularly provides executive coaching support for senior leaders and undertakes examination marking for the CIPD.

Krystal Wilkinson is currently a Doctoral Student at Leeds University Business School, in the Division of Work and Employment Relations, and is also an Associate Lecturer at both Leeds University and Manchester Metropolitan University Business Schools. She has been on CIPD exam-marking teams for several years and has recently been involved in authoring Workbooks for the CIPD Flexible Learning resource. Prior to returning to academia, Krystal had several years' operational HR experience in a range of sectors including construction, hospitality and retail.

CHAPTER 1

Human Resource Service Delivery

Gail Swift

CHAPTER CONTENTS

- Introduction
- The changing context of HR service delivery
- Models of HR service delivery
- Challenges to the Ulrich model
- Outsourcing HR services
- The delivery of HRM by line managers
- Measuring the impact of HR services
- Recent developments in HRM service delivery
- Conclusion

KEY LEARNING OUTCOMES

By the end of this chapter, you should be able to:

- understand the reasons why organisations change the structure and location of HR service provision by analysing the changing context of human resource service delivery
- critically evaluate different models of HR service delivery available to contemporary organisations
- critically discuss the reason for measuring the impact of service delivery and the measurement indicators used
- understand recent thinking on HR service delivery.

INTRODUCTION

One of the key variables in achieving the aims of HRM is way the service is delivered. We know from studies of contingency variables in organisations and management that no two organisations utilise the same functional structure and involve the same levels and roles of staff in delivering HRM. Each HRM department is subject to different forces, producing a unique approach to HR service delivery. Our purpose in this chapter is to focus on delivery models of human resource management and the way it delivers its product to the organisation with particular reference to structures and roles.

Over the past two decades the role and structure of the HR function in organisations has been debated and, some claim, undergone a process of transformation. Dave Ulrich's ground-breaking model of human resources services delivery in his book *Human Resource Champions: The next agenda for adding value and delivering results* (1997), spurred many senior HR leaders to structure and restructure the delivery of their services to meet the challenges of changing national and international business conditions. Ulrich offered a powerful re-interpretation of the personnel function, which outlined the significance of HR as a change agent in championing competitiveness in US firms (Caldwell, 2001). At the time he argued that the role of the HR professional must be redefined to meet the competitive challenges organisations were facing then and would face in the future (Bentley, 2008).

This chapter begins with a further consideration of some of the reasons why organisations have changed the structure and location of HR service provision. It then explores the models that are available to contemporary organisations to deliver HR services. It looks at Ulrich's 'three-legged stool' model in some detail and debates the question whether its implementation has met with success. It also looks at other models of delivery that are evident in organisations, including the use of outsourcing and external consultants. It goes on to consider the role of the line manager in HR delivery and how organisations have sought to devolve HR practices to line managers in order to support a shift to a more strategic level of practice for HR professionals. How HR services are measured and evaluated is then discussed. Finally, the chapter concludes with a look at recent thinking on the future of HR service delivery – in particular at the recent research by the CIPD into **'insight-driven'** HR and the impact that this may have on how HR services are delivered over the coming years (CIPD, 2011e).

THE CHANGING CONTEXT OF HR SERVICE DELIVERY

No two HR departments are configured in the same way to deliver their service, even though they share the same predominant aim. The 2006 CIPD report *The Changing HR Function* concluded that the primary driver for the **structural transformation** of HR has been the desire for the function to be a more strategic contributor and to maximise HR's contribution to business performance. Business leaders have also come to perceive the link between talent management and business success and to recognise HR's potential role in unlocking the discretionary effort of employees as a source of competitive advantage.

The link between HR and customer service has strengthened over recent years, with those in the vanguard of change moving to increase the value HR offers to its business customers (CIPD, 2006). HR has been charged with developing and organising 'human capital', and the ways in which employees are recruited, developed and managed are seen as key to this. Employees' satisfaction has been recognised as an important factor in delivering effective services, and many organisations now recognise the link between well-organised and well-managed teams and business success.

The project to deliver value through HR has met with varying degrees of success. The majority of organisations now have an HR director on the board. However, despite a presence at the top table and an express desire to be seen as an equal strategic partner in the business, there still appears to be considerable debate over whether there is definitive evidence of the impact of HR structures and staffing on organisational performance (CIPD, 2006). What is clear, though, is that current business conditions demand a greater delivery of competitive advantage via HR agendas and practices, and require HR to have true strategic influence that is internally coherent with the values of the business and aligned to its goals and objectives (Becker and Huselid, 1999). It may be concluded therefore that the way in which HR is structured to deliver its services is a key factor in determining its operational success.

REFLECTIVE ACTIVITY

Consider your organisation or one that you are familiar with. How is HR delivered? Is it delivered in partnership with other organisations or are certain activities totally outsourced to expert organisations such as consultants? In particular, how involved are line managers in the delivery of HR services?

This question pivots firstly on the extent to which the organisation you are considering retains in-house HR expertise, and secondly on the nature of the relationship between the HR function and the organisation's line managers. Each organisation is different and the models of delivery are affected by variables such as:

Organisation-level factors

- Organisation size: larger organisations are likely to utilise more innovative features of delivering HRM – for example, more partnerships, shared arrangements and outsourcing.
- Sector: private sector organisations are also more likely to consider arrangements such as those listed above
- History, traditions and structure: bureaucratic, layered, staid and static

organisations, which may also have a longer history and maturity to them, are more likely to have a traditional line-manager-associated delivery mode
- Culture of the organisation – such as the difference between organisations that encourage decision-making at a low structural level and those that are paternalistic and more supportive.

HR-level factors

- Level of organisational representation and responsibility for input into strategy – it is suggested that outsourced transactions, for example, can give the HR manager more time for strategic input
- Size of department
- The history and traditions of HR operations.

Personal factors

- The power, influence and perspective of the HR manager/director
- Their experience and background
- The CEO's previous experience of HR.

MODELS OF HR SERVICE DELIVERY

How HR is structured to deliver its services has been the subject of considerable debate and discussion over recent years. A variety of ways in which HR functions have been organised have been examined. As was explained in Chapter 1 of the book *Studying Human Resource Management* in this series (Taylor and Woodhams, 2012), whether services should be organised on a best-practice basis or a best-fit basis is at the centre of much of the debate. Research carried out by the CIPD highlighted the views of practitioners that HR should be structured to reflect the business that it is in and what its business customers want (CIPD, 2006). What emerges from the literature are two approaches to HR structures that dominate the way in which services are currently organised, which are discussed in further detail in this section of the chapter:

- traditional approaches of a single team of generalists, specialists and administration, or a corporate strategy team aligned by business units or locations
- the 'three-legged stool' model of business partners, shared services and centres of expertise.

TRADITIONAL HR STRUCTURES

A traditional structure of HR services, consisting of a single team with generalists, specialists and administration, is still common in many organisations. In this type of structure, an integrated HR team generally looks after line managers and employees at specific locations or within specific units of the business. Within these teams, depending on their size, there may also be specialisation by work area or by employee grade or group (CIPD, 2006). HR staff in these structures may look after administrative and clerical staff as opposed to managerial grades, or look after technical specialties – for example, medical staff in the NHS. Evidence from the 2011 CIPD autumn outlook suggests that this is still the most common structure for HR functions. This model of HR delivery appears to be particularly prevalent among small and medium-sized organisations (SMEs), 64% of respondents in the report stating this to be the case in medium-sized organisations and 47% in small organisations (CIPD, 2011c). This is due to the fact that because of resource constraints, HR teams in SMEs have to be versatile and deal with both the strategic and the operational work. Smaller and less complex organisations in particular (in a single location and with a homogeneous population) continue to have generalist HR staff covering a range of tasks (CIPD, 2006).

A similar study from Crail (2006) of the HR function in 179 UK organisations concluded that a 'standard' HR department might typically have the following characteristics:

- It would have a team of 12 people serving a workforce of around 1,200.
- This team would consist of an HR director, three HR managers, one HR supervisor, three HR officers and four HR assistants.
- The department would spend a lot of its time on HR administration, despite some activity as a 'business partner' and strategic contributor.

- Attempts would have been made to shift some HR responsibilities to line managers, not always successfully.
- The department would enjoy some influence over the way the organisation was run and HR's standing in the organisation would be generally high, partly because the external contexts have changed and HR is seen as the source of knowledge and expertise on legal and regulatory requirements.

As this piece implies, the connection between the HR function and operational managers can be fraught. The HR department might attempt to shift HR responsibilities because doing so is in line with a model of ownership and buy-in from managers to the goals of HRM. But managers are reluctant to embrace these responsibilities. We investigate this issue later in the chapter.

ULRICH'S 'THREE-LEGGED STOOL' BEST PRACTICE MODEL

Over recent years it has been Ulrich's model of human resource services delivery – commonly referred to as the 'three-legged stool' model or the 'three box' model – which has become regarded as best practice, although there is 'ongoing debate about how his theories should be interpreted and put into practice' (CIPD, 2011a: 1). The most common interpretation of the model is based on three means or mechanisms of service delivery: HR business partners, HR centres of expertise, and shared HR services. These are discussed in turn in more detail in the following sections.

HR business partnering or strategic partners

The CIPD states that HR business partnering is the process in which HR professionals work closely with business leaders and/or line managers to achieve shared organisational objectives. Business partners are senior or key HR professionals. They are usually embedded in the business unit where they work in partnership with operational managers within that business unit to influence and steer strategy and strategy implementation. Research has found that the role of business partners varies widely between organisations, with factors such as 'organisational size, company culture and business priorities' appearing to determine how the business partner role is carried out (CIPD, 2011a: 1). In the 2006 CIPD survey, 83% of organisations reported that they had introduced Ulrich's business partner model in some way.

The benefits of the business partner role appear to be that it allows the HR practitioner to become a more strategic contributor, with increased business focus, greater engagement with line managers and the ability to move people management issues higher up the business agenda (Reilly, Tamkin and Broughton, 2007). When HR professionals are embedded in business units, research appears to suggest that they are able to more easily select and implement HR practices that are most appropriate to developing the business strategy for that unit. This structure allows HR partners to utilise their 'unique' knowledge and skills to support and drive change in people management practices. They can also be well placed to support local managers in considering the people consequences of changes to strategy or policies (CIPD, 2011a; Ulrich, Younger and Brockbank, 2008). HR business partners can also work with line managers on longer-term people resourcing and talent management planning issues. Their role in intelligence-gathering and understanding of good people management practices, internally and externally, enables business partners to raise issues which managers may be unaware of (CIPD, 2011a).

Although many professionals have welcomed the move to a more strategic role, there have also been challenges to this approach. Pritchard (2010: 183) suggests that the transition from generalist to business partner has often not been easy for HR professionals, who can find it 'difficult to step away from day to day activities, in which they had been involved for many years'. Whereas the business partner role has 'given freedom from previous generalist work and enabled a more strategic focus', Pritchard (2010: 181) has observed that in some cases business partners continued to remain involved in generalist work. Some practitioners, however, feel that this is an 'essential stepping stone' to a more strategic role (Pritchard, 2010: 184). Being able to understand how the **transactional** side of the agenda works and having the ability to continue to resolve HR issues was regarded as essential to building trust with line managers. This was seen by some practitioners involved in the study as a prerequisite to successful partnerships (Pritchard, 2010). Obtaining people with the right levels of skills and credibility to perform the role of business partner was also cited as an issue with introducing business partnering to organisations (Reilly, Tamkin and Broughton, 2007). Ulrich, Younger and Brockbank (2008) suggest that a new competence of 'strategic architect' is required for the role, which in essence means 'embedded HR professionals being able to diagnose what needs to be done; broker resources to get things done; and monitor progress to ensure things are accomplished' (Ulrich, Younger and Brockbank 2008: 842). This new skill set, together with a perceived natural reluctance to give up an area of work that had previously been seen as adding value (Pritchard, 2010), suggests that the introduction of business partnering has not been without its difficulties. Despite this, research has shown that business partnering remains an attractive role for HR practitioners and organisations (CIPD, 2003).

Centres of expertise

Centres of expertise in Ulrich's model usually comprise 'a team of HR experts with specialist knowledge of leading edge HR solutions'. The role of centres of expertise is to 'deliver competitive business advantage through HR innovations in areas such as reward, learning, engagement and talent management' (CIPD, 2011a). Evidence of implementation of centres of expertise suggests that they are accessed on a corporate, regional or national basis. In the 'three-legged stool' model they offer their services either to HR business partners or in some circumstances directly to line managers (CIPD, 2007). They often act like businesses in themselves and can have a number of business units using their services. In some organisations some method of internal recharging for these expert services and products is used.

Ulrich, Younger and Brockbank (2008) suggest that the role of the HR professional in centres of expertise covers a number of important areas, notably in creating **menus of intervention** aligned with the capabilities required to drive the strategy for the business forward:

- diagnosing needs and recommending the most appropriate solution
- working collaboratively with HR business partners to select and implement the right services
- researching and creating new offerings
- acting as guardian of the learning community within an organisation.

There are also some risks inherent with operating centres of expertise that must be guarded against. They include:

- relying on programmes that the centres are familiar with but that are not tailored to the needs of individual business units
- isolation from day-to-day business, so that solutions can appear to be out of touch with the reality of the business
- a tendency to 'craft single solutions' (Ulrich, Younger and Brockbank, 2008: 844), which are then applied to numerous business units
- excessive demands placed on the centre by working for numerous business units, each business unit believing that its own demands are the most important and the most deserving of an immediate response
- an assumption that in creating a centre of expertise business units will be happy to use them. In some organisations line managers and business partners are required to access the central expertise before seeking outside help, but in others managers may pick and choose between the central service and external consultants, especially if there is a high degree of devolved budgets for learning and support activities.

Shared services

The CIPD's definition of shared services is based on a single, often relatively large, unit that handles all the routine 'transactional' services across the business. This features recruitment administration, payroll, absence monitoring and advice on simpler employee relations issues. The remit of shared services is to provide low-cost, effective administration (CIPD, 2011b). Shared services emerged in the late 1990s as HR leaders realised that many administrative tasks could be performed in a centralised, standard way (Reilly, 2000). Its introduction has frequently been one element of a wider restructure of HR services, often associated with the introduction of the three-legged stool service model.

Reilly (2000) found that there were three principal reasons for the introduction of shared services – cost, quality and **organisational change** – development in technology being the facilitator of the movement to shared services rather than the driver for it. The 2007 CIPD survey *The Changing HR Function* found that just over a quarter of organisations had introduced a centralised provision of shared administrative services. Typically, these services are located in-house although they can be outsourced to specialist third-party providers (see the section on outsourcing later in the chapter). Often the use of shared services centres is also associated with the move to devolve people management activities from the HR department to individual managers or employees by the use of **self-**

service technologies. The benefits of shared services reflect many of the reasons why organisations looked to implement them in the first place (Reilly, 2000):

- lower costs
- more efficient resourcing
- an improved quality of service
- increased customer satisfaction
- a single point of contact
- an integrated 'total solution' approach
- greater transparency of costs
- more consistent management information
- economies of scale for investment in technical and communications infrastructure
- the release of time to spend on strategic issues.

CIPD (2007) research has identified shared services as a phenomenon of large rather than small organisations, two thirds of organisations employing over 5,000 employees citing that they have some degree of shared services, as opposed to 17% of organisations that employed 250–1,000 staff. The research cites several high-profile private sector companies that have recently entered into shared service arrangements and an increased interest in take-up in the public sector.

To demonstrate this idea in practice, an interesting case study illustration is reproduced below of how a joint venture between Liverpool City Council and BT delivered HR services in a new way. Evidence in the case suggests that through a radical overhaul in providing services and the appointment of a new HR leader, the joint venture has been useful in providing HR services that:

- are more cost-effective
- are united behind a single product
- provide HR jobs that are varied and skilled
- free up in-house provision to focus on strategic matters
- build joint commitment to solutions
- construct green shoots of a commercial model that can offer services to other organisations.

 HR services and the joint venture: Liverpool City Council and BT

CASE STUDY

When David Henshaw took over as chief executive of Liverpool City Council in October 1999, he had his work cut out. The Council was third from bottom in the local authority performance league table, with only the London boroughs of Hackney and Lambeth deemed to provide poorer services for their residents. Not only that, Liverpool also had the most expensive Council Tax in the country.

His brief was to cut costs and bureaucracy, stabilise the Council Tax and improve services and information for the local community and the Council's staff. Henshaw set in motion a modernisation process that saw the authority's eight directorates condensed down to five portfolios, a new executive team and 2,700 jobs shed – 10 per cent of its workforce.

He also focused his attention on what he saw as one of the major obstacles to delivering better services and value for money – the Council's inefficient business processes. The state of the HR function at the time provides a good example. It was split into eight units, each providing day-to-day operational support for a directorate, plus one central corporate unit. The eight units were basically doing the same job, but all had a different way of doing things and had their own interpretation of corporate policies.

'There were 200 people in HR, but it wasn't a good service,' Henshaw says. 'Personnel officers in different units were spending their time arguing with each other about different versions of the truth.'

Henshaw's aim was to get down to one version, not only for HR but for the whole Council, and to ensure that everyone had access to it. To do this, the Council's information and communication technology (ICT) needed considerable improvement. ICT had been underfunded for years. But the Council's previous outsourcing experience had not been encouraging.

'Outsourcing can and does go wrong,' says Henshaw. 'You can outsource a problem and end up with an outsourced problem, rather than a solution.' Instead, he took a different approach and started looking for a private-sector partner to form a joint venture with.

In May 2000 BT was chosen as preferred bidder to help run the business support services, and Liverpool Direct Limited (LDL) was born. BT would invest £60 million in the company over a 10-year period, and provide the much-needed computer systems and software. The Council would pay the company £330 million to run all its business support (including

ICT, HR and payroll) and its front-line customer services, such as benefits and advice services. All these services would be restructured to benefit from the technology. This would allow mundane processes to be automated and information to be shared, saving time and money.

The HR department was to play a major part in the change to the new model. First, it would be involved in the overall restructuring, handling the redundancies, overseeing the selection of executive directors and recruiting the second tier of assistant executive directors. Second, it would go through a fundamental transformation, taking on a new structure and ways of working as it became part of LDL.

A new HR management team of seven was set up, and the old system in which each HR team supported a single directorate [akin to a department] was scrapped. In its place four new teams based on expertise (employment relations, resourcing, learning and development, and payroll and pensions) were formed.

The redundancy programme was judged a success: the target of losing 10 per cent of the workforce through voluntary redundancy was achieved. HR is now part of LDL, and the latest stage of its transformation has been the launch of the intranet, allowing all staff and line managers to access HR policies and other information online, and the opening of the HR service centre, which went live in January 2001.

Although 81 per cent of LDL is owned by BT and 19 per cent by Liverpool City Council, Henshaw stresses that the Council is in the driving seat in terms of the direction and management of the company. In fact, beyond providing the hardware, BT's involvement seems to be limited to advice on setting up and running business service administration systems. The staff who are actually providing the services have all come from the Council and were already working in similar areas. They have been seconded to the company but, crucially, are still employed by Liverpool City Council.

For Henshaw the joint venture is a positive way of accessing private money and know-how without the disadvantages of outsourcing. 'Our sector has to think differently about what it does, and move away from stale outsourcing deals,' he says. 'When outsourcing goes wrong, people reach for the lawyers rather than working to solve the problems. In our contract with BT we have very clear targets for service improvements and cost reductions, and we have to work together to achieve those.'

He adds that LDL has plans to provide services for other authorities. The extra business would bring in revenue for the Council, as well as BT, and create more jobs. They are currently in discussion with two authorities.

'There are few private companies that have managed to make this work on their own,' he says. 'The public sector has a huge amount to contribute. If we can harness that with the private sector, that's good for everybody.'

Liverpool Direct Limited's HR service centre handles telephone enquiries and, where necessary, refers callers on to someone with greater expertise in the back office. The intranet and service centre have removed the burden of process-related tasks from the 70 back-office staff.

Front-line call centre staff were previously HR administrators and say the change in role has been a positive one. Customer services adviser Peter Lynskey says that the job is more varied and has given him new computer skills.

The new structure has also freed up the HR management team. HR project manager Mike Evans, who was responsible for setting up the intranet, was previously manager of one of the HR units – a job that had little impact on the Council at large or the community. Now the projects he runs are all about improving the way the Council works and the services it delivers.

'LDL has opened up opportunities for people throughout the organisation to do things with real scope,' he says.

Adapted from Hammond (2002)

CHALLENGES TO THE ULRICH MODEL

A great deal of the debate over the past 15 years, since Ulrich first introduced the concept of business partnering, has centred on the perceived success of the model within business and the extent to which it has enabled HR practitioners to adopt a more strategic approach. Pitcher (2008) argues that the business partner model has not resulted in strategic thinking, and is little more than superficial 'spin'. He cites the example of Elizabeth Arden, in which the HR director, Gabriele Arend, disagreed with any model that splits HR professionals into recruiting, training and employee relations experts. Her company is moving towards a traditional structure, where HR employees are trained to develop generalist operational knowledge. The CIPD (2010) recommends exercising caution when adopting the business partner model and suggests that partnering should mean a paradigm shift for most HR functions, resulting in changes to HR's values, operation and skills, and not simply a repackaging of good HR practice. Perhaps the key question comes down to HR's credibility and contribution, summed up succinctly in a Deloitte Report (2009: 8):

> The business partners' greatest failing has been their inability to convince senior managers that they have the necessary business acumen to contribute to the strategic debate.

Similar findings in research conducted by the Roffey Park Institute into the use of business partners revealed that 55% of HR professionals thought that it had been a success but 32% remained unsure, with a further 10% claiming that it had not been successful at all in their organisations (Hennessey, 2009). Reilly, Tamkin and Broughton's work for the CIPD (2007) found a wide variety of ways in which organisations have implemented this model, and which differed greatly from the textbook version outlined in Figure 1.1.

Figure 1.1 Variants in implementation of the three-legged stool model

A large number of business partners and a shared service centre but no centres of expertise because business partners are expected to be conversant with most HR issues	A small number of HR teams, led by a business partner, a support unit/shared service centre and a policy strategy unit	A corporate HR function, an insourced shared services operation and a well-staffed business unit
Business partners for each of the main departments, and centres of expertise – including an employment support line – which pick up the administrative work; a shared payroll operation but no shared service as such	A small number of business partners – one for each department – a policy unit, a separate learning unit and a development design unit, a call centre, a 'duty desk', case work section and a project team; administration is carried out by a shared service centre located outside HR	Business partners, together with learning and development advisers embedded in business units, with a corporate 'service delivery' unit and a strategy consultancy group
Shared services (where appropriate globally), business partners (aligned to global business units, regions or individual locations) and centres of expertise	Business partners, an advisory call centre, a global shared service centre and different levels of centres of expertise at global(principles and strategy), regional (guidance on implementation) and local level (actual delivery)	Business partners, regional administrative service centres, together with call centres but with payroll executed locally, no centres of expertise but with core HR strategy units and delivery teams

Source: Reilly, Tamkin and Broughton ([CIPD], 2007: 13–14)

Despite the undoubted popularity of Ulrich's model, many commentators remain sceptical as to its true success and unconvinced of it as 'the right way forward for people management'. Some critics have maintained that it has all too often only involved a 'change of title only' for HR managers (Hennessey, 2009: 26) and has not resulted in any improvement in strategic thinking on HR issues within business (Pritchard, 2008). Ulrich claimed, however, that poor implementation and a lack of understanding had let the model down (Peacock, 2008). Real concerns were expressed that many practitioners have rushed into implementing the Ulrich model without properly considering whether it met the needs of the business first. Where the Ulrich model has been introduced, it is the business partner leg of the stool that has proved the most popular, whereas centres of expertise and shared services are less frequently found (CIPD, 2007).

Conclusions to be drawn from the research suggest that there is not a one-size-fits-all model, and many commentators have drawn attention to the need for structure to follow strategy. To quote from a CIPD survey (CIPD, 2007: 19):

> The Ulrich model is useful – but adapt it to your circumstances.

OUTSOURCING HR SERVICES

According to the CIPD Executive Briefing (2005), this is the practice of transferring some, or all, of the HR service provision from an in-house team to one or more external providers. It is also utilised by a number of small organisations that, unable to carry their own internal resource, form an agreement to finance a common service to which they all have an equal, or agreed, access. HR services may be transferred on an anticipated long-term basis, or may be outsourced for the completion of a specific piece of work or project (CIPD, 2005).

There has been significant growth in this type of external provider, firms such as Capita, Accenture, Hewitt and Exult taking large chunks of HR business. To illustrate, the case study below taken from *People Management* (2006) announces a BBC deal with Capita.

Capita wins BBC's HR outsourcing contract

CASE STUDY

Capita has won a ten-year contract to manage the BBC's HR services.

Under the contract, Capita will deal with BBC staff recruitment, pay (excluding pensions), occupational health and other services including some training and development. The work will be handled by Capita's Belfast office and will create 100 new jobs in the city.

'This deal marries both our expertise in HR with the resource and expertise of a leading player in business process outsourcing,' said Stephen Dando, director of BBC People. 'The value created from this deal is a significant step for us in ensuring that the BBC continues to invest in creating innovative programmes and services for our audiences.'

The BBC claims it will save more than £50 million over the ten-year contract period.

The decision on whether or not to outsource HR services is debatable and contentious in literature and practice. A typical outsourcing arrangement allows HR services for an organisation to be transferred out of ownership of the organisation to a third-party supplier to be re-provided back into the organisation. Alternatively HR services are purchased outright from a specialist firm, such as Capita in the UK, who offer such services. Typically, these are the transactional elements of services.

REASONS FOR OUTSOURCING DECISIONS

Organisations usually decide on an outsourcing option for one or more of the following reasons:

- It can enable access to specialist skills and knowledge not possessed by the in-house team and which the outsourcing organisation is unable or unwilling to develop for it.
- It can be seen as a means of achieving levels of service quality and efficiency, which, for one reason or another, are not considered to be achievable within the outsourcing organisation itself.
- There may be an anticipation of significant savings on an ongoing basis, which is attractive to any organisation seeking to reduce its overall costs.

According to the 2009 survey on outsourcing activity conducted by the CIPD (2009a), the incidence of outsourcing extended to around 29% of the survey respondents and was said to be increasing, especially over the five years prior to the study. Outsourcing appeared to be most prevalent in the private sector, around 69% of the survey respondents engaging in the practice. It was apparently less common among public service organisations, where it extended to only 25% of the respondents.

The survey also demonstrated a clear link between organisational size and outsourcing activity. Large organisations, with more than 10,000 staff, outsourced up to 71% of at least some of their HR activity, retaining 29% in-house. Smaller organisations, employing fewer than 250 staff, retained only 11% for provision on an internal basis.

HR outsourcing is most commonly used in the transactional and specialist functions. Typically, these are recruitment, training, pensions, payroll, legal services, information systems and compensation and benefits. All of this, taken together with the findings in the preceding paragraph, fits neatly with the reasons why organisations opt to engage in outsourcing, outlined in the bullet points above.

SKILLS REQUIRED BY HR PRACTITIONERS IN OUTSOURCING DECISIONS

HR outsourcing is perceived to require a particular set of skills and knowledge on the part of those involved in the process. These include the ability to properly plan, specify and cost the services that are to be provided externally. Thereafter, the process requires that contracts have to be made, tendered, awarded and then monitored carefully on an ongoing basis if the expected benefits are to be achieved and maintained. According to the 2009 CIPD survey, HR professionals involved in outsourcing considered themselves as having the necessary level of competence in those areas deemed to be important. However, vendor management – which involves partnership working, together with an understanding of the way in which commercial organisations operate on a day-to-day basis – was not regarded as crucial to a successful outcome. The survey in fact indicated that HR professionals only ranked this fifth in terms of importance. Further, 13% of HR outsourcers lacked vendor management skills and 6% lacked any financial skills.

The stated results of HR outsourcing seem to be quite mixed. If the intended objective was to outsource the transactional elements of HR activity to allow an in-house concentration on strategic work, the findings show that this appears not to have been the result (CIPD, 2009). Only 11% of the respondents reported that this had happened – 54% indicated some movement towards a more strategic involvement, while 36% reported no development in strategic activity at all.

In general, only 11% of the survey respondents considered that HR outsourcing had been a success; 47% reported success in some areas but not in others, and the remainder said that success had not occurred, had been limited, or that it was too early to tell.

The general conclusion is that HR outsourcing does have a place within the provision of HR services, but that to ensure that it is successful it must be carefully planned and targeted. It must be aimed at those areas where it can make a viable contribution, and it must be well monitored once it is in operation. HR outsourcers must have developed the necessary skill sets required for successful engagement, and outsourcing must be regarded positively as an integral and strategic aspect of HR activity generally.

THE DELIVERY OF HRM BY LINE MANAGERS

Line managers have taken increasing responsibility for the delivery of HR practices over the last few decades and now play a critical role in people management in most organisations. Significantly, the way line managers implement these practices can influence employee attitudes and behaviour. Line managers are therefore the important link between employee experiences of HRM and the formation of their attitudes towards their job and the organisation. Line managers have appropriately been called 'HR agents' of the organisation because they mediate between individuals and HR practices (Truss, 2001). Research from Crail (2004) makes it clear that first-line managers are increasingly expected to have the solution to everything, from absence management to productivity. The research listed 23 areas of responsibility and asked respondents whether these were the responsibility of first-line managers alone, a shared responsibility, or not their responsibility at all. Only a handful of the 62 employers contacted said that the following had nothing to do with line managers:

- absence management
- appraisals
- grievance
- health and safety
- planning/allocating work
- recruitment
- staff deployment
- team briefing
- team development
- ongoing training
- welfare.

This is similar, at headline level, to a similar survey issued in 2000, although there has been a substantial increase in the number of organisations identifying each of these areas – and a still greater increase in those saying that these areas are now the sole responsibility of line managers. So a great deal is expected of first-line managers who are already busy dealing with operational responsibilities. This trend looks set to continue, many respondents expecting line managers to become more autonomous and take on more responsibility, especially for people management.

The importance of line managers in the delivery of HRM, however, is far greater than a quantitative survey can reveal. The work of Appelbaum *et al* (2000) and Purcell *et al* (2003) emphasises that the likelihood of employees' engaging in discretionary effort is influenced by the role of line managers. For example (Appelbaum *et al*, 2000: 235):

> plant managers who invest in the skills of front-line managers and include these workers in decision-making activities elicit discretionary effort by employees. This effort increases operational efficiency and competitive advantage.

This is an important conclusion. It suggests that there is a direct link between line management training and the willingness to work beyond contract and 'go the extra mile' on the part of employees.

 REFLECTIVE ACTIVITY

Reflect on your organisation or one you know well. Which people-related issue is the most common source of tension between line managers and the HR function? Why do you think this is the case?

MEASURING THE IMPACT OF HR SERVICES

Why measure HR performance? It could be said that on one level the effectiveness of – or the necessity for – HR activity speaks for itself. Clearly, if an organisation cannot recruit, retain, develop and deploy its staff efficiently, it will not survive. But this, in itself, is not enough of a contribution. The HR function has to show that it is part of the general movement towards greater efficiency and cost reduction. This in turn demands the development of viable measurement processes and techniques with which it can demonstrate its effectiveness.

This is particularly important given the pressures under which modern organisations now operate, with an increasing emphasis on good business practices, the development of new technology and the extensive use of management information systems. Customer and stakeholder requirements have become sharper and much more closely defined, which gives providing organisations increasingly less room for manoeuvre. Inefficient practices cannot be concealed or buried and so must be identified and addressed.

The HR function must therefore, in so far as it is possible, seek and apply ways of indicating efficiency, if it is to achieve and maintain any degree of credibility in the organisation in which it operates.

MEASUREMENT INDICATORS

The measurement of human resource efficiency may be somewhat difficult, and indeed thought by some not to be possible at all (Brewster and Tyson, cited in CIPD, 2005). There are, however, a number of measures that can at least move towards a greater understanding of the contribution of HR to overall organisational effectiveness. These range from the general to the more specific and quantitative.

Overall, general tests of HR effectiveness rely firmly on the extent to which HR objectives are directly linked to the aims of the organisation as outlined in its strategy and its associated operational plans. If this is well done – that is to say, if the workforce plan is developed along with the organisational strategy and seen as integral to it and not as a post-planning 'add-on' – then it may be said to be effective if the organisation as a whole is seen to be succeeding. This of course is a somewhat indirect measurement of HR effectiveness, but is nonetheless considered to be viable.

If, for example, the organisational strategy demands a workforce of a particular character and shape, possessing a defined skill mix, and the HR function is able to provide this through effective recruitment, retention, training, development and employee relations policies, then it must be seen to be making a valuable contribution. This descends from the introduction and maintenance of sound HR policy and procedure at the senior level to a committed application on the ground with a rigorous attention to detail, fairness and consistency. A good example of HR outcomes in practice is found in research reports from Michael West *et al* (2006) who strongly suggest that good HR practices can be seen to affect the performance of hospitals, as evidenced through a reduction in the mortality rate.

In a study of 61 hospitals in England the researchers (from the Institute of Work Psychology at Sheffield University) found strong associations between HR practices and business performance measured through patient mortality. The Chief Executive and HR directors completed a questionnaire asking them about their hospital characteristics, HRM strategy, employee involvement strategy and practices, and other HR policies and practices covering the main occupational groups, such as doctors, nurses and midwives, professions allied to medicine, ancillary staff, professional and technical staff, administrative and clerical, and managers. Data was also collected on the number of deaths following emergency and non-emergency surgery, admissions for hip fractures, admissions for heart attacks, and re-admission rates. Care was taken not to bias the data and account was taken of the size and wealth of each hospital and of the local health needs. In particular, the researchers found that:

- appraisal has the strongest relationship with patient mortality
- the extent of teamworking in hospitals is also strongly related to patient mortality
- the sophistication of training policies is linked to lower patient mortality.

Specific and quantitative indicators include the use of **staff turnover** and **stability figures**, sickness absence rates, the incidence of discipline and grievance cases and personal performance and appraisal outcomes. These provide strong clues to the overall health of an organisation from which the motivation and commitment of the workforce directly stems.

Making comparisons through **benchmarking** these and other indicators between organisations can indicate relative efficiency or otherwise. Care must be taken, however, to ensure that correct and valid comparisons are being made and that there is due regard to any operational, structural or cultural differences that may affect the outcomes.

Other measures may include the study of response rates in the recruitment and grievance-handling process, customer and stakeholder feedback, both formal and more casual, **employee engagement** and output, and the detailed costing of HR activity with which to make informed decisions on the way in which HR services should be provided. That is on an in-house or external basis.

It may be difficult to determine the right balance between specific and more general HR performance measures, or indeed choosing the right ones to use in the circumstances – not made any easier by the existence of over 1,000 human capital indices (Hartley and Robey, cited in CIPD, 2005). The most important thing is to ensure that these are tailored to the needs and character of the organisation (CIPD, 2005).

Once established and used, HR performance indicators both general and specific should be kept under continuous review in order to ensure their ongoing value and effectiveness. Used positively and confidently, good HR indicators may be a powerful determinant in the direction taken by the organisation as a whole and in the credibility of the HR function in particular.

REFLECTIVE ACTIVITY

Carefully read the following quotation from Angela Baron's conversation with Max Blumberg, Research Fellow at Goldsmiths, University of London, taken from the CIPD podcast on *Using metrics to drive value through people* (1 February 2011). Angela is the CIPD's Organisation Development and Engagement Adviser.

She agrees with Max Blumberg that HR measurement is a discipline that is becoming more sophisticated, and states that:

'Measuring has come along a great deal in the last ten years or so. We've seen a move from organisations where they struggled to even find out how many people worked for them, to where organisations are now mostly in a situation where they're pretty comfortable with data; where they're able to access some data which gives them some indications about things like skill levels, about skill shortages, about how difficult or how easy it is to recruit, some information about the culture, maybe, how satisfied people are, how engaged they are, performance data, etc. Where the difficulties are found is in translating that data into real measures that are linked to business outcomes.'

Now see if you can answer the questions that appear below. Log on to the CIPD website to hear the discussion on the podcast in more detail if you have the opportunity.

1   Why might organisations have struggled to make use of measurement data in the past?

2   What measure of HR services is used in your organisation (or an organisation that you are familiar with)?

3   If you were to design a 'dashboard' of metrics for your organisation (or an organisation that you are familiar with) to show how HR measures are linked to business outcomes, what would your dashboard look like? What are the reasons behind your choice of performance metrics?

Source: *Using Metrics to drive value through people* (2011) CIPD Podcast http://www.cipd.co.uk/podcasts, 1 February

RECENT DEVELOPMENTS IN HRM SERVICE DELIVERY

This chapter has discussed the models of HRM service delivery that are currently found in operational practice, and has concentrated on discussion of the results of research and academic thinking that demonstrate their relative effectiveness.

The CIPD Next Generation Research (2010) work, however, challenges us to think about where the HR profession is headed, and has identified a need for HR to move away from 'the service delivery and process focus with which HR is typically identified' to be more *insight-driven* (CIPD, 2012b: 2). This research focuses on the need for HR practitioners to become 'business-savvy' and to develop a much deeper understanding of the business within which they operate. The popularity of Ulrich's model stemmed in part from the desire of HR professionals to become more closely aligned with the business. Models of shared services, centres of expertise and outsourcing have allowed HR practitioners to concentrate their efforts at a more strategic level. This recent research suggests, however, that 'a comparable deeper shift in mindset and focus' is now required (CIPD, 2011e: 5). It observes that a good deal of current HR practice is still strongly concerned with service and process delivery. 'Getting things done' with 'intervention-led delivery and high-volume activity' is still seen as the measure of success for many HR and business leaders (CIPD, 2011e: 5). It proposes that HR practitioners will need to become:

- business-savvy: having a deep understanding of a business's core values and drivers – a deep appreciation of what makes the business successful or not
- context-savvy: having an understanding of market trends and forces that affect the business and an understanding of the broader macro-economic and societal factors that affect organisations both now and in the future
- organisation-savvy: having a rich understanding of how hard and soft factors interplay to enable or derail business success – a deep understanding of change dynamics and the impact of people, culture and leadership.

Insight, it suggests, is 'not currently on the agenda for the conscientious HR professional'. The report concluded that the profession will need a significant shift 'similar to that from a policing style to business partnering' if the profession is to 'evolve again to offer organisations what they need to move to a sustainable future' (CIPD, 2011e: 5). How this research will impact on the future structure by which HRM services are delivered remains to be seen, and has the potential to be the source of debate much as that raised by Ulrich's model 15 years ago.

CONCLUSION

This chapter has highlighted key elements of the way an organisation structures its HR service delivery. At the start of the chapter the context in which HR services are delivered was explored. A range of variables that impact on the delivery of HR services was considered. Following on from this, the current models of HRM service delivery were explored, with a particular focus on a discussion of the introduction of Ulrich's three-legged stool model as opposed to the continued use of more traditional HR structures, together with a consideration of its success or otherwise. This section concluded that no one-size-fits-all model appears to be evident from the research, even though the Ulrich model has recently been considered to constitute best practice. The introduction of HR business partners appears to remains a popular method of HR service delivery. This has allowed the HR function to become more closely aligned with business practice. The chapter went on to look at HR outsourcing and its place in the provision of HR services. In particular, it focused on its role in supporting HR to realign its services as an aid to cost reduction and to concentrate resources on strategic issues within the organisation. Towards the end of the chapter we reviewed the connection between line managers and HR services. We also analysed the measurement of HR services, including their accompanying methods, and concluded that, used well, good HR indicators may be a powerful determinant in establishing the credibility of the HR function. The chapter ended with a look at a potential challenge to the way HRM services may be delivered in the future, involving a glimpse of the CIPD's Next Generation research into *insight-driven* HR.

FURTHER READING

CIPD (2005) *HR Outsourcing: The key decisions*. London, Chartered Institute of Personnel and Development (Scott-Jackson, W., Newham, T. and Gurney, M.).

CIPD (2006) *The Changing HR Function: The key questions*. London, Chartered Institute of Personnel and Development (Tamkin, P., Reilly, P. and Strebler, A.).

CIPD (2007) *The Changing HR Function: Transforming HR*. London, Chartered Institute of Personnel and Development (Reilly, P., Tamkin, P. and Broughton, A.).

CIPD (2011) *Next Generation HR: Insight-driven*. London, Chartered Institute of Personnel and Development.

Reilly, P. (2000) *HR Shared Services and the Realignment of HR*. University of Sussex, Institute of Employment Studies.

Ulrich, D. (1997) *Human Resource Champions: The next agenda for adding value and delivering results*. Boston, MA, Harvard Business Review Press.

REFERENCES

Appelbaum, E., Bailey, T., Berg, P. and Kalleberg, A. (2000) *Manufacturing Advantage: Why high performance systems pay off*. Ithaca, NY, ILR Press.

Becker, B. and Huselid, M. (1999) 'Overview: strategic human resource management in five leading firms', *Human Resource Management*, Vol.38: 287–301.

Bentley, R. (2008) 'Where did the business partner model go wrong?', *Personnel Today*, 26 March.

Caldwell, R. (2001) 'Champions, adapters, consultants and synergists: the new change agents in HRM', *Human Resource Management Journal*, Vol.11, No.3: 39–52.

CIPD (2005) *HR Outsourcing: The key decisions*. London, Chartered Institute of Personnel and Development (Scott-Jackson, W., Newham, T. and Gurney, M.).

CIPD (2006) *The Changing HR Function: The key questions*. London, Chartered Institute of Personnel and Development (Tamkin, P., Reilly, P. and Strebler, A.).

CIPD (2007) *The Changing HR Function: Transforming HR*. London, Chartered Institute of Personnel and Development (Reilly P., Tamkin, P. and Broughton, A.).

CIPD (2009a) *HR Outsourcing and the HR Function: Threat or opportunity*. London, Chartered Institute of Personnel and Development.

CIPD (2009b) *HR Outsourcing*: Factsheet. London, Chartered Institute of Personnel and Development.

CIPD (2011a) *HR Business Partnering*: Factsheet. London, Chartered Institute of Personnel and Development.

CIPD (2011b) *HR Shared Services Centres*: Factsheet. London, Chartered Institute of Personnel and Development.

CIPD (2011c) *HR Outlook*. Autumn. London, Chartered Institute of Personnel and Development.

CIPD (2011d) *HR Outlook*. Spring. London, Chartered Institute of Personnel and Development.

CIPD (2011e) *Next Generation HR: Insight-driven*. London, Chartered Institute of Personnel and Development.

CIPD (2012a) *Barometer of HR Trends and Prospects*. London, Chartered Institute of Personnel and Development.

CIPD (2012b) *Business Savvy: Giving HR the Edge*. Research report – phase 1. London, Chartered Institute of Personnel and Development.

Crail, M. (2004) 'Welcome the multi-tasking all-purpose management expert', *IRS Employment Trends*, No.793, February.

Crail, M. (2006) 'HR roles and responsibilities 2006: benchmarking the HR function', *IRS Employment Review*, No. 839, January: 9–15.

Deloitte (2009) *Shaping Up: Evolving the HR function for the 21st century*. New York/London, Deloitte MCS.

Economist (2102) *The World in 2012*. London, The Economist.

Hammond, H. (2002) 'A dynamic duo', *People Management*, 21 March.

Hennessey, J. (2009) 'Take your partners and advance', *People Management*, 29 January: 24–7.

Peacock, L. (2008) 'Dave Ulrich's model defence', *Personnel Today*, 15 April.

People Management (2006) 'Capita wins BBC's HR outsourcing contract', 17 February.

Pitcher, G. (2008) 'Backlash against HR business partner model', *Personnel Today*, 29 January.

Pritchard, K. (2010) 'Becoming an HR strategic partner: tales of transition', *Human Resource Management Journal*, Vol.20, No.2: 175–88.

Purcell, J., Kinnie, N., Hutchinson, S., Rayton, B. and Swart, J. (2003) *Understanding the People and Performance Link: Unlocking the black box*. London, Chartered Institute of Personnel and Development.

Reilly, P. (2000) *HR Shared Services and the Realignment of HR*. University of Sussex, Institute of Employment Studies

Reilly, P., Tamkin, P. and Broughton, A. (2007) *The Changing HR Function: Transforming HR*. Research into Practice. See CIPD (2007).

Taylor, S. and Woodhams, C. (2012) 'Studying HRM', in S. Taylor and C. Woodhams (eds) *Studying Human Resource Management*. London, Chartered Institute of Personnel and Development.

Truss, K. (2001) 'Complexities and controversies in linking HRM with organizational outcomes', *Journal of Management Studies*, Vol.38, No.8: 1121–49.

Ulrich, D. (1997) *Human Resource Champions: The next agenda for adding value and delivering results*. Boston, MA, Harvard Business Review Press.

Ulrich, D., Younger, J. and Brockbank, W. (2008) 'The twenty-first century organisation', *Human Resource Management*, Winter, Vol.47, No.4: 829–50.

Vanson, S. (2001) *The Challenge of Outsourcing Human Resources*. Oxford, Chandos.

West, M. A., Guthrie, J. P., Dawson, J. F., Borrill, C. S. and Carter, M. R. (2006) 'Reducing patient mortality in hospitals: the role of human resource management', *Journal of Organizational Behavior*, Vol.27: 983–1002.

Wetherly, P. and Otter, D. (2008) *The Business Environment: Themes and issues*. Oxford, Oxford University Press.

CHAPTER 2

Employment Law

Stephen Taylor and Krystal Wilkinson

CHAPTER CONTENTS

- Introducing UK employment law
- Recruiting and promoting people
- Change management
- Pay and working time
- Managing discipline and poor performance
- Other major employment rights

KEY LEARNING OUTCOMES

By the end of this chapter, you should be able to:

- understand the purpose of employment regulation and the way it is enforced in practice
- manage recruitment and selection activities lawfully
- manage change and reorganisation lawfully
- manage issues related to pay and working time lawfully
- ensure that staff are treated lawfully when they are at work
- manage performance and disciplinary matters lawfully.

INTRODUCING UK EMPLOYMENT LAW

In recent years it has become essential for HR managers to gain and then to maintain a good working knowledge of employment law. This is because the amount of employment law has increased greatly alongside the willingness of people to take their cases to an **employment tribunal**.

There are now over 80 distinct types of claim that can be brought to an employment tribunal, in addition to many more that are employment-related but that are heard in the county courts (Shackleton, 2005). Many of the most important of these have either been introduced or expanded in the past ten years (e.g. discrimination on the grounds of age, religion or belief and sexual orientation, paternity leave, rights for agency workers, etc), giving people more potential grounds for launching legal claims. Employers have also contributed by sacking more people. It is estimated, for example, that 2.7 million people were made redundant during the economic downturn between 2008 and 2012, receiving severance payments of £28.6 billion (CIPD, 2012). The impact on the tribunal system has been huge. In 1990/91, 43,244 cases were lodged with the UK employment tribunal system. Twenty years later, in 2010/11, the number was 218,000 (ETS, 2011).

Employment law can affect and influence a huge range of HR decisions, policies and practices. It requires us to think carefully before going ahead with plans that make complete operational sense but that carry a legal risk. It restricts what we are able to do in practice and accounts for a great deal of our time – 20% on average, according to a CIPD survey (2002).

Employment law is also the subject of a great deal of debate and fierce political controversy. This is because people disagree hugely about its economic benefits and about how far it is in practice desirable to protect employment rights through state regulation.

DEBATES ABOUT EMPLOYMENT LAW

The arguments in favour of extensive employment law are rooted in the desire to enhance social justice. While we tend to presume that employers and employees are equal parties, free to negotiate contractual terms as they see fit, this is a long way from being the reality of the position for most. In truth, employers are many times more powerful than their employees and in a position, should they wish to, to exploit them unreasonably. Were it not for employment law, many employers would be tempted to compromise on health and safety, to pay unfairly low wages, to work their staff far too hard, to sack them for no good reason without compensation and to deny them basic rights such as maternity leave and equal pay for men and women. Minority groups would have fewer opportunities than they do, while all would run the risk of being bullied and harassed by unscrupulous managers. There would also be few guaranteed rights for **trade unions** and their members, and no obligations on employers to consult with their staff about anything at all.

The main arguments against employment regulation are economic. It is argued that although protections of this kind undoubtedly benefit employees, there is a price to pay in higher unemployment and lower economic growth. Employment law places a 'regulatory burden' on employers, often takes the form of unnecessary red tape, and hugely increases the economic risks associated with employing people. It thus serves to act as a major deterrent to smaller employers who might otherwise hire new people and to international companies who choose not to site their operations in the UK because the conditions are more employer-friendly elsewhere. More generally, because employment law adds to

UK employers' costs, it makes them less competitive than commercial rivals based in other countries.

Another set of arguments against employment regulation is based on the idea that it actually harms the people it is intended to protect. It is not uncommon, for example, to hear of instances in which prominent business people argue against employing women of child-bearing age because of the many employment rights that they have the potential to claim (Lea, 2001; Brewer, 2008).

Less commonly expressed, but equally important, are the economic arguments in favour of employment regulation. Some argue, for example, that it is important to make work attractive in order to make sure that employers have access to the skilled staff that they require and who otherwise might choose to take early **retirement** or work in another country. It is also persuasively argued that poor, inequitable employment practices reduce employee commitment and hence productivity. The most productive and efficient economies in the world, it is pointed out, are often the most highly and effectively regulated ones.

 REFLECTIVE ACTIVITY

The groups that complain most about the negative impact of employment regulation have always been those who represent the interests of small businesses. They argue that larger organisations can cope much better with it because they have more resources available and because employment law tends to be designed around their needs. This often leads them to argue that there should be major exemptions for small businesses from whole areas of employment law.

1   Why are small businesses less well equipped to deal with increasing amounts of employment regulation than larger ones are?

2   What arguments can be made against the proposition that small businesses should not be required to comply with some employment laws?

THE EMPLOYMENT LAW SYSTEM

Most UK employment law takes the form of **statutes** passed by Parliament. These comprise Acts (e.g. the Employee Relations Act 1996, the Employment Act 2002, the Equality Act 2010) or Regulations issued under the terms of Acts (e.g. the Working Time Regulations 1998, the Agency Workers' Regulations 2011, the Unfair Dismissal and Statements of Reasons for Dismissal Regulations 2012).

In recent years many employment statutes have had a European origin, the UK Parliament giving effect in British law to the contents of Directives agreed by European Union institutions.

It is, however, important to grasp that not all of our employment law appears in statutes. Indeed, some of the most significant rights have never been considered by Parliament, let alone made by it. Instead, they come to us via the **common law**, which has been made by judges and which has evolved over many centuries.

This is true of the law of contract, which regulates the fundamental relationship between employers and employees, and of the law of negligence, which provides us with the right to claim compensation when we suffer an injury at work. The common law is made when judges rule on points of principle in cases that are brought before them. These then become precedents, which are followed whenever a similar case is brought in the future.

The UK court system is hierarchical, there being a right to appeal against the outcome of cases to a higher court. Because the rulings of higher courts on points of law are binding on all the lower courts, new law is effectively created whenever a higher court decides that the law is to be interpreted in a particular way. This principle applies when it comes to the interpretation of statutes as well as in common law matters. The practical consequences are highly significant. It means that UK employers have to be familiar not just with what a statute says, but also with what it has been held to mean in practical terms in the case law.

As a rule when **claimants** (employees, ex-employees or failed job applicants) wish to pursue claims that concern rights enshrined in an employment statute, they lodge their claim at their local employment tribunal office. A few months later, provided the claim is neither withdrawn nor settled, a hearing will be convened at which both sides in the dispute present their cases, cross-examining one another's witnesses and asking the presiding Employment Judge to interpret the law in their favour. In some circumstances a panel of three may hear a case, but nowadays it is more common for cases to be heard and decided by judges sitting alone.

For most areas of jurisdiction, **employment tribunals** are only able to accept a case and list it for a hearing if the claim form arrives at the tribunal office within three months of the incident about which the claimant is complaining. In the case of contested dismissals the cut-off date is three months from the date at which the dismissal took effect (the effective date of termination). In the case of ongoing disputes the rule is that a case must be brought within three months of a date at which it is alleged a detriment was suffered by the claimant. So, for example, an employee who believes that he or she has not been paid at the level of the National Minimum Wage has up to three months from their leaving date to pursue a claim.

Appeals from the employment tribunal can only be made on points of law. You cannot appeal simply because the judge found your witnesses to be less credible than those of your opponents or because of the way particular facts were interpreted. However, if you believe that the judge has misapplied or misinterpreted the law – case law as well as statutes – an appeal can be made to the next court in the hierarchy. This is the **Employment Appeals Tribunal** (the EAT), which has responsibility for interpreting how new employment statutes will be interpreted, and thus makes highly significant rulings that affect all employers in the country.

Disputes that relate to the common law do not generally go before an employment tribunal. Instead, they are heard by judges of the County Courts or, when high levels of compensation are being sought, by the High Court. Here no three-month rule applies, most claimants having up to six years to bring a claim before they are timed out.

Appeals from the EAT, County Court and High Court are heard by the Court of Appeal in England or the Court of Session in Scotland. It is rare for cases go further, but when major issues of public interest are at stake, cases can be appealed to the **Supreme Court** (formally known as the House of Lords). This happens in an employment matter perhaps three or four times a year. The Supreme Court is the final court of appeal as far as UK law is concerned. However, when a case concerns a principle of European law there is the possibility of a further appeal to the **European Court of Justice** in Luxemburg. This is where disputes about the implementation and interpretation of EU Directives are settled.

RECRUITING AND PROMOTING PEOPLE

HR managers are obliged to take account of the possible legal consequences of their actions across all areas of their activities. The law permits people who have a range of 'protected characteristics' to claim compensation when they suffer from unfair discrimination. So when recruiting, selecting and promoting staff, managers need to ensure not only that they treat everyone who applies for a job equitably and fairly, but also that they are seen to do so.

Another area of employment law that has to be taken account of when recruiting new staff is the law of contract. When a new employee is hired, a **contract of employment** is established, which is legally binding on both parties and enforceable in the courts. Importantly, this means that employers are not lawfully able to alter someone's pay or employment conditions unilaterally without first securing their agreement. So it is essential that great care is taken to offer terms that will subsequently be honoured.

DIRECT AND INDIRECT DISCRIMINATION

The Equality Act 2011 provides protection from unfair discrimination for people with the following protected characteristics:

- age
- disability
- gender reassignment
- marriage and civil partnership
- pregnancy and maternity
- race, ethnicity and national origin
- religion or belief
- sex
- sexual orientation.

In addition, further EU law provides some protection for the following groups:

- part-time workers
- fixed-term workers.

Further UK law also extends some protection on the following grounds:

- being ex-offenders
- union membership or non-membership.

In the case of the protected characteristics covered by the Equality Act, a clear and important distinction is made between direct and indirect discrimination. Direct discrimination occurs at the recruitment stage when an employer fails to shortlist or to appoint a well-qualified person purely on grounds of a protected characteristic. Appointing a woman because she is a woman, or a white person because of his or her ethnicity would be examples of direct discrimination. In the case of most protected characteristics, actions such as these, if they are proven on the balance of probabilities to have occurred, are unlawful. In other words, the case goes against the employer and compensation must be paid to the claimant. Importantly, no defence can be heard. However reasonable or justified an employer considers its actions to have been, rejecting a candidate on one of these grounds is simply not lawful.

There are nonetheless some exceptions to this general rule. Firstly, it is lawful for employers to reserve some jobs for particular groups. These are jobs that have what are known as 'occupational requirements' (formerly 'genuine occupational qualifications'), which mean that they have to be done by people of a particular gender, race or age. Acting and modelling jobs are common examples, as is work in ethnically themed restaurants and where, for reasons of decency, a job can only practically be carried out either by a man or a woman. Secondly, in the case of discrimination on grounds of disability and age (and not the other protected characteristics), employers are entitled in law to deploy a general justification when they directly discriminate. In other words, an employer can argue that a disabled person was turned down for a job on grounds of disability or that a 65-year-old was turned down on grounds of age, but that there is a good, genuine business reason that justifies the decision. In the case of disability discrimination the tribunal must be satisfied that there are no 'reasonable adjustments' to working practices or to the working environment that the employer could make in order to accommodate the needs of a disabled candidate. In the case of age discrimination the following question is asked:

> Did the decision not to appoint/shortlist/promote the claimant amount to a proportionate means of achieving a legitimate aim?

This same legal test is used to determine cases of indirect discrimination, although here the defence can be deployed in the case of all the protected characteristics. An act of indirect discrimination occurs when an employer has in place 'a rule, criterion or practice' that has an adverse effect on a substantially greater number of people with a protected characteristic than it does on others.

A simple example is a height requirement. Were an employer to state that applicants for a particular role had to be over six feet tall, it would be applying a rule that many more men are able to comply with than women. That is indirect discrimination. The same of course would be true in reverse were an employer to stipulate that only people under six feet could apply for a role. Indirect race discrimination in recruitment occurs when an employer stipulates that it will only consider applications from people who hold a specific UK qualification, while indirect religious discrimination occurs when an employer requires staff who are prepared to work on religious holiday days. Indirect age discrimination is most common of all, happening whenever a person specification requires a set number of years' experience before a job application will be considered. This is because fewer younger people are able to comply with the condition than older people. In all of these cases the employer is acting unlawfully unless it can satisfy the tribunal that its rule, criterion or practice represents 'a proportionate means of achieving a legitimate aim', namely that there is a good, genuine business justification for it.

The Equality Act also permits employers to discriminate positively in favour of 'under-represented groups' when they are recruiting, but only in circumstances in which they have interviewed candidates who are equally appointable. So an organisation with no women on its board of directors could, if it wished to, select a female candidate over a male rival provided the two were of equal merit. The reason given could, quite lawfully, be that she was chosen because she is a she.

REFLECTIVE ACTIVITY

Which of the following recruitment decisions, in your view, would be lawful, which unlawful, and why?

- Only shortlisting people of Chinese ethnicity to work as waiting staff in a Chinese restaurant
- Stipulating that cabin crew employed to work on an aeroplane must be under six and a half feet tall
- Refusing to interview a man aged 55 who has applied to join a company's graduate training scheme
- Turning down an application from a disabled woman who, while well qualified, could only perform the job in question if she is assisted by other employees in doing so
- Insisting that all applicants for a teaching job in a Roman Catholic school are baptised Roman Catholics
- Selecting a well-qualified male candidate for employment as a primary school teacher because all the existing staff are women and a more balanced team is sought
- Only recruiting people to a driving job who can demonstrate that they posses 'a full, clean UK driving licence'.

FORMING A CONTRACT OF EMPLOYMENT

Discrimination law of the kind described above generally applies to all workers, whatever their contractual status. However, this is not true of all employment law, some of which applies only to people who are employed to work under 'contracts of service', commonly known as 'contracts of employment'. This includes the right not to be unfairly dismissed as well as a host of other important protections that employees enjoy thanks to the law of contract, such as the right to a relationship of mutual trust and confidence. Moreover, of course, once a contract of employment is established, it cannot generally be altered without both sides agreeing to an amendment.

For these reasons managers must take great care when recruiting staff to ensure that both sides are fully aware of the type of relationship they are entering into and the legal rights and obligations that it entails.

Establishing a contract of employment is remarkably easy. There is no need for any written documentation or even a handshake. A contract can be formed during a telephone conversation or via an exchange of emails. Obviously, it is preferable for the main terms and conditions to be spelled out unambiguously on paper so that everyone knows where they stand, but this is not a prerequisite in UK law for the establishment of a legally binding contract. In fact there are only five major conditions that must be in place in order for a contract of employment to exist:

- an unconditional offer
- an unconditional acceptance of the offer
- an intention to form a legal relationship (i.e. not an informal agreement between friends and family members)
- consideration (payment or payment in kind)
- certainty (i.e. clarity about the main terms and conditions).

One or two further regulatory restrictions ensure that minors are not bound to contracts that operate against their interests, that the contract is not 'tainted by illegality' and that both parties are 'of sound mind' when the contract is formed. It is also important to note that 'consideration' is not always a requirement under Scottish law. Otherwise, provided all five conditions are satisfied, a contract of employment exists with all the legal rights and obligations that follow.

Some types of contractual arrangement between workers and their employers are defined in law as amounting to 'contracts for services' rather than 'contracts of service'. These are not full contracts of employment and mean, as we explained above, that the job-holder does not enjoy the full protection of all employment law.

The distinction between 'a contract of service' and 'a contract for services' is not always clear. Self-employed people can fall into the second category, but do not always do so, giving rise to further complications about who exactly has what legal rights and about when and where they can be enforced.

We do not have the space in this chapter to discuss these complex legal issues at any length. You will find a proper, full explanation of the situation in Taylor and Emir (2012: Chapter 3). But it is important that you appreciate one key point. When deciding who falls into which category, the courts look at the reality of the relationship that has been established between the worker and the employer. It is not possible to deny people their full employment rights simply by labelling the relationship 'self-employment', 'an agency contract' or 'casual employment' and providing documentation to that effect. Employers are often tempted into this in order to avoid paying employers' National Insurance contributions (a payroll tax on employees paid by employers), but they are often acting unlawfully in doing so. As far as the law is concerned, what matters is what happens in practice. If a worker works under the control of an employer and uses its tools for the job, cannot substitute someone else when he or she cannot work and cannot turn work down if it is offered without risking losing the job, there is in all likelihood a contract of employment in place with all that this entails legally for both parties.

CHANGE MANAGEMENT

Here too great care must be taken in order to avoid breaching employment law and running the risk that staff (or former staff) will seek damages for compensation in court. Managers need to take particular care to avoid pushing through changes in terms and conditions unlawfully, but it is also necessary in many cases of reorganisation to take account of redundancy law and the Transfer of Undertakings (Protection of Employment) Regulations.

CHANGING CONTRACTS LAWFULLY

As we explained above, a core principle of the law of contract in the UK is that once formed, a contract of employment is legally binding on both parties. An employer cannot lawfully make changes without first securing the agreement of the employee any more than the employee can announce a unilateral change. However, the law recognises that from time to time employers have to make changes for good, strong business reasons. We do not have the space here to discuss all these situations in depth, but the following are the most important and the most common:

- Including a flexibility clause in the contract that gives the employer the right to make reasonable changes to terms and conditions from time to time in accordance with business needs. Mobility clauses are a common form of flexibility clause, which allow employers lawfully to re-locate their staff provided reasonable notice is given.
- Writing to the employee setting out contractual changes, while anticipating that there will be no negative response. This is an uncertain approach but can work if the employee's response is to continue to come to work without objecting to the change. There is no specific time stipulation, but after two months or so an employer is entitled in law to assume that the employee has signalled 'acceptance through practice'.
- Negotiating changes with a trade union when there is a collective agreement in place that has been incorporated into all individual contracts of employment.
- Dismissing staff before rehiring them instantly on new terms and conditions of employment. This is a risky option because it raises the possibility that employees will bring unfair dismissal cases and, if successful, require reinstatement of their original contracts. Sometimes, however, there is no choice if contractual change is to be forced through against the wishes of affected employees. The key is to remember that in doing this the employer must act 'reasonably' if it is to defend itself successfully in court. Usually this means only moving to 'dismissal and rehire' as a last resort.

Employers are entitled in law to make technical changes to working arrangements that fall short of contractual amendments. This includes the introduction of new machinery or of new working practices provided they do not impact on core contractual terms such as hours of work or pay rates. It is also important to remember that a breach of contract claim will only succeed if a claimant can satisfy the court that a genuine detriment has been suffered. Causing staff relatively minor inconvenience is therefore unlikely to lead to a court case – as, of course, are changes that on balance work in the employee's favour, such as pay rises.

A final point to make in this section concerns the law of **constructive dismissal**. This can only be claimed by employees with over a year's service behind them (two years if their employment started after 6 April 2012), but they can win substantial compensation if successful. A constructive dismissal occurs when the following conditions (set in the case of *Western Excavating (ECC) Ltd v Sharp*, 1978) are all satisfied:

- The employer must, through its action, be in actual or anticipatory breach of the contract of employment.
- The employer must be guilty of 'a significant breach going to the root of the contract' or show through its action that it no longer intends to be bound by an essential term of the contract.
- The employee must decide to resign shortly after the breach.
- The employee must resign in response to the breach.

This means that an employee who chooses to resign rather than to accept an employer's breach of contract is able to pursue their claim for compensation at the employment tribunal and is not required to go to the County Court at considerable expense. Employers can defend themselves in cases of constructive dismissal by demonstrating that a reorganisation was necessary for a good business reason and otherwise carried out reasonably, but there are considerable, potential financial risks associated with failing to satisfy the tribunal that this is the case.

REDUNDANCY

A well-established employment right that applies to all employees who have completed two years' service is the right to receive a severance payment when they are made redundant. There are also a range of procedural requirements that employers must follow when making redundancies in order to avoid claims of unfair dismissal.

A **redundancy** occurs when an employer is reducing its headcount for economic reasons. People are dismissed, albeit with compensation, because the employer can no longer afford to continue their employment. While individual conduct and performance may well determine who is selected for redundancy and who continues to work, these are not the reason that the dismissals are occurring.

Redundancies are part and parcel of many change management episodes. It is not difficult to carry them out lawfully when you know what you are doing, but this does not prevent many thousands of cases going to the employment tribunal each year. The key requirements are:

- The employer must identify a pool of 'at risk' employees from whom it will select those who are going to be made redundant. The decision about who should and should not be in the pool is for the employer to determine, but it must be reasonable.

- The employer must consult with those who are at risk about the proposed selection method and about ways of minimising the number of redundancies. Individual consultation is always required. Collective consultation with a recognised trade union or other elected representatives is required when more than 20 redundancies are proposed.
- Redundancy selection must be objective and reasonable. In practice this means either selecting those who have the shortest service ('last in, first out'), scoring everyone according to performance measures or requiring 'at risk' staff to apply competitively for jobs in a new structure.

Minimum levels of redundancy compensation are set out in the employment statutes. These increase somewhat each year, but are based on the employee's age, length of service and current salary. At the time of writing (2012) the maximum payment that employees can claim under the statutory scheme is £12,000. In practice many employers pay considerably higher sums, particularly when they are contractually obliged to do so.

TUPE

The Transfer of Undertakings (Protection of Employment) Regulations derive from two European 'acquired rights' Directives dating from 1977 and 2001. In the UK the law in this area has long been referred to as 'TUPE' (pronounced 'tupey'). It is complex and unsatisfactory in many ways, although matters were clarified to an extent with a new set of Regulations that came into effect in April 2006.

The aim of the law is to help ensure that in most respects employees do not lose out when the identity of their employer changes, and to protect them from dismissal or redundancy when a business transfer takes place. TUPE now applies in two distinct types of situation:

- where a business, part of a business or part of another type of employing organisation is merged with or taken over by another employer
- where the contract to provide a service is either lost by one provider and won by another, or otherwise outsourced/insourced by an organisation.

The TUPE Regulations thus have to be taken account of in many cases of structural change, in any situation in which the identity of someone's employer changes, or when a contract that a group of staff work on most of the time transfers from one provider to another.

The key employment rights/legal duties that apply in TUPE situations are:

- Employees affected by a transfer have the right to be consulted formally before, during and after the transfer by both the transferor and transferee organisations.
- Employees have the right to have their continuity of service recognised by their new employer.

- The contents of contracts of employment transfer with the employees to whom they apply. It is usually unlawful to force changes to contracts as a result of a TUPE transfer.
- Employment-related liabilities and benefits as well as collective agreements transfer along with employees in TUPE situations.
- It is usually unfair in law to dismiss an employee for a reason related to a TUPE transfer.
- There are obligations placed on transferors to give specific information to transferees about the employees who are transferring.

The TUPE Regulations are usually seen as providing important legal rights protecting the interests of employees. It is important to remember, however, that in one very major respect they favour the employer's interest. This is because they deny employees the right to object to being transferred across to another employment except where the regulations are not fully complied with. If an employee does object and resigns at the point of transfer, however many years' service he/she has, there can be no case for unfair dismissal or constructive dismissal unless there is a reduction in the level of terms and conditions (i.e. TUPE is not followed) after the transfer.

PAY AND WORKING TIME

How much we are paid and the amount of work we do are for most people the most significant elements of their contract of employment. They are also fundamental factors in determining our productivity and hence our value to our employers. They are therefore key sources of potential conflict between staff and their organisations and are, unsurprisingly, regulated quite heavily in important respects.

THE NATIONAL MINIMUM WAGE (NMW)

Since 1999, each year, a body called the Low Pay Commission has advised ministers on an appropriate level for the NMW. It is required to recommend a wage that will maximise living standards for the lowest-paid workers but which is not so high as to have a serious adverse impact on levels of employment.

In fact the government sets four separate minimum hourly rates for different groups of workers. In most years these rise on 1 October. At the time of writing (early 2012) the rates are:

Main adult rate:	£6.08
Lower rate for those aged 18–22 or 22+ who are in training in a new job:	£4.98
Youth rate for 16–17-year-olds:	£3.68
Apprentice rate:	£2.60

The main adult rate is scheduled to increase to £6.19 an hour from 1 October 2012.

EQUAL PAY LAW

One of the longest-established employment regulations stipulates that men and women should be paid the same for doing 'like work, work which is rated as equivalent and work of equal value', provided they work for the same employer, the same group of companies or are covered by the same industry-level collective agreement. This right is enshrined in the major European treaties and is generally considered to constitute a fundamental human right. The law in the UK has a number of complexities that can be confusing, but the fundamental rights are easily stated and readily explained.

The term 'like work' means any work that is either the same or broadly similar. So two people, one male and one female, should be paid the same amount for doing the same job. 'Work of equal value' refers to a situation in which a man and a woman are employed in the same organisation but do different jobs. The law states that if the work they do is nonetheless broadly equal in terms of the level of skill, experience and effort required, as well as the level of responsibility the jobs carry, then their pay should also be the same. Where this is not the case, a mechanism is provided for a claimant to test his or her case at an employment tribunal. Provided a basic case can be made out, the tribunal is obliged to appoint an 'independent expert' to carry out a job evaluation exercise to determine whether or not the two jobs are of equal value.

The term 'work rated as equivalent' requires more explanation. This plays a part when an employer carries out a job evaluation exercise which results in two different jobs (one held by a man, the other by a woman) being graded at the same level. Sometimes an employer will do this but will then stop short of implementing the new grading system. In such cases a claim can be made to enforce equality. More commonly, work rated as equivalent cases relate to situations in which a new grading system is introduced, resulting in a group of employees being regraded to a higher level thanks to a job evaluation exercise. If the group is predominantly female, for example, and now finds itself graded at the same level as a group which is predominantly male but which has historically been paid more, then claims for back pay can be made going back for six years.

Employers can defend themselves in equal pay cases by satisfying the tribunal that there is a good, genuine business reason that explains any pay differential between men and women who should, on the face of it, be paid equally under the terms of equal pay law. These are known as 'material factors', the most significant of which are:

- one worker has more/higher qualifications than the other
- one worker is more skilled or has undertaken more training than the other
- one worker is more productive or higher-performing than the other
- one worker has greater seniority/length of service or experience than the other
- regional allowances (e.g. London weightings) explain the difference in pay
- the shift patterns are different – one worker being prepared to work more unsocial hours, for example
- budgetary constraints at the time of appointment meant that it was not possible to afford to match salaries between the male and the female worker.

DEDUCTIONS FROM WAGES

The right not to have unauthorised deductions made from your pay packet applies to all workers, not just to employees. It is small and simple bit of law but one that accounts for 20% of all employment tribunal cases. Essentially, the law lays out clearly the circumstances in which an employer *can* make deductions from pay without the consent of the worker. It follows that it is unlawful to make deductions in any other situation. The situations are:

- to recover overpayments of wages
- where a court orders that a deduction is made (e.g. an attachment order)
- when a worker takes industrial action
- where it is authorised by legislation (e.g. tax)
- where it is authorised by contract (e.g. trade union dues).

There are special rules for retailers to deal with cash shortages/stock deficiencies and for the police and army that permit fines to be levied as part of disciplinary procedures. The regulations do not permit fining for disciplinary offences in 99% of organisations. Fines cannot therefore be levied (i.e. for lateness, misconduct, damage to property, etc) unless:

- there is an express term of contract saying it is permitted

or

- the employee has agreed in writing *in advance* of the incident.

SICK PAY, MATERNITY PAY, ETC

These regulations help ensure that employees who are unable to work for periods due either to sickness, maternity or paternity are nonetheless paid a reasonable daily rate through their employer's payroll for set periods of time. In the case of Statutory Maternity Pay (SMP) and Statutory Paternity Pay (SPP) employers can claim back much of the money from the government through reduced National Insurance contributions. At the time of writing (2012) the rates are:

Statutory Sick Pay (SSP):	£81.60 per week
Statutory Maternity Pay (SMP):	90% of salary for the first six weeks of maternity leave, then £128.73 for the remaining weeks.

Statutory Paternity Pay and Statutory Adoption Pay (for parents of newly adopted children) are paid at the same level as SMP.

Some groups do not qualify – mainly people who work part-time and earn too little. They have to claim money from the Benefits Agency instead.

It is important to understand that these are the statutory minimum sums that have to be paid by law. In practice many employers offer much more generous arrangements as part of their benefits packages. Return-to-work bonuses are also relatively common in the UK but are not required by law.

THE WORKING TIME REGULATIONS

These originate in the European Union and are quite complex and lengthy. However, the basic fundamental rights they give are easily summarised:

- a limit of 48 hours' work per week
- four weeks' paid annual leave each year in addition to the eight statutory bank holidays
- 20 minutes' rest in any period of work lasting six hours or more
- 11 hours' rest in any one 24-hour period
- 24 hours' rest in any seven-day period
- night workers are limited to eight hours' work in any one 24-hour period and have the right to free, regular health checks
- special provisions that restrict the working time of young workers (i.e. 16–18-year-olds).

On the surface this looks clear-cut and straightforward, but this is in fact far from the case. The Regulations are very complex, running to more than 100 pages in length. There are three types of situation in which some or all of the Regulations do not apply. The major sources of complexity are:

- averaging
  The regulations allow for considerable flexibility because they allow employers to average time worked over a reference period – in most cases 17 weeks.
- opt-outs
  More generally, anyone can if they wish formally 'opt out' of the 48-hour week restriction by signing or writing a written declaration. Employers in the UK are lawfully able to make the signing of such an opt-out a requirement of employment.

  Anyone is entitled at any time to opt back in by informing their employer in writing – they have to give three months' notice and cannot be victimised for exercising this right.
- workforce agreements
  These allow an employer to seek to vary Working Time Regulations in various ways if it first secures acceptance by its workforce through a workforce agreement. Effectively, this means that whole workplaces can adapt their interpretation of the Working Time Regulations to suit their needs.

MATERNITY LEAVE

The statutory scheme specifies three different types of maternity leave:

- ordinary maternity leave (OML)
- compulsory maternity leave (CML)
- additional maternity leave (AML).

OML applies only to employees, but there is no qualifying period of service. It is now 26 weeks in duration (i.e. six months).

OML normally starts on the intended date – i.e. on the date the employee informed the employer that it would start. The earliest it can start is the 11th week prior to the Expected Week of Confinement (EWC) – that is, the date on which the baby is expected to be born.

However, it starts automatically at an earlier time in certain situations:

- if the baby arrives early
- if the woman is absent owing to a pregnancy-related illness in the four weeks prior to the EWC.

CML is straightforward: it is simply the two weeks after the birth, during which there is now a compulsory period of maternity leave. The onus is on the employer to make sure that no work is done during this period. Normally, CML and OML overlap – the baby would have to arrive extraordinarily late for this not to be the case – so CML only applies where a woman decides she does not wish to exercise her right to OML. The EU is currently actively considering a proposal to extend CML from two weeks to six weeks. It is too early to say whether or not such a change is likely to happen and, if so, from what date.

There is a general right of return to the same job on the same terms and conditions following CML and OML, all pay rises and other improvements to terms and conditions being honoured. After the return to work, the contractual situation should be as if the maternity leave had not happened. The only exception is where the job becomes redundant during OML, in which case the right is to return to a suitable alternative job with similar terms and conditions.

It is important to remember that the right is to return to the same *job* and not necessarily to the same work. It may be that changes have been made in the woman's absence that mean the work that she does on her return may be somewhat different. It only becomes a different job if the content is substantially altered. At present there is no general right for a woman to return on a part-time basis or on different working hours unless this is provided for in the contract of employment. But there is just a right to request flexible working, and a requirement that the employer only turns down such requests for defined business reasons set out in the statutes.

AML (additional maternity leave) applies only to employees (i.e. women working under a 'contract of service') and it runs for a further 26 weeks following on from the end of OML.

The right to return after AML is to the same job *if reasonably practicable*. Otherwise, it is to a suitable job on no less favourable terms and conditions.

During maternity leave the contract of employment continues in all respects except for pay. All benefits continue to accrue (including holidays). Company cars, portable computers and mobile phones are kept, health insurance is retained and all duties owed by employers and employees (mutual trust and confidence, etc) continue.

Since 2007 employers have gained the right to maintain reasonable contact with employees who are on maternity leave. This is to discuss a range of issues – e.g. their plans for returning to work, or to keep them informed of important developments at the workplace. The employee should also be informed of any relevant promotion opportunities or job vacancies that arise during maternity leave. In addition it is now possible for a woman to return to work on a temporary basis, by mutual agreement, for up to 10 days during her maternity leave in order to 'keep in touch', without this bringing the leave to an end. Pay for these days is something that is left for the individual parties to agree.

PATERNITY AND ADOPTION LEAVE

Fathers of newborn babies have a statutory right to take ordinary paternity leave (OPL) at the time of the birth, the right applying to employees who have been employed for 26 weeks at the start of the 14th week before the EWC and who expect to have responsibility for the child's upbringing. The period is up to two weeks, and it must be taken within 56 days of the birth.

Additional paternity leave (APL) was introduced in 2011. Under this scheme mothers are able to return to work after taking 20 weeks of maternity leave, passing on up to a further six months to their baby's father. APL is paid for three months at the lower rate of Statutory Maternity Pay (SMP) unless employers have alternative arrangements in place for paying women more during their AML.

The right to return after the leave is the same for fathers taking APL as it is for mothers taking AML, as is the right to retain contractual benefits such as cars, laptops and even live-in accommodation.

Parents who adopt children are permitted under the statutory scheme to take leave on the same basis as parents of newly born children. The key date here is that on which the match between parents and child was made. The big difference is that the couple can choose which of them is going to take maternity leave and be paid SMP and which will take the benefits associated with paternity.

FURTHER FAMILY-FRIENDLY EMPLOYMENT RIGHTS

In addition to the rights to take leave that are associated with maternity, paternity and adoption, there are one or two other statutory rights that apply in UK workplaces. These are:

- the right to take unpaid time off work to deal with family emergencies
- the right to take four months' unpaid parental leave
- the right to request flexible working.

The latter right permits employees, once a year only, to write to their employer formally asking for a one-off change in terms and conditions, together with an explanation as to how his or her request could be accommodated. Any change made as a result of the request is both contractual and permanent. So, for example, there is no right to request a year's part-time work followed by a return to full-time working.

The employer can turn the request down if it believes there is a good business reason for doing so. There are eight possible reasons given in the statute for legitimately refusing a request:

- the burden of additional costs
- a detrimental effect on the company's ability to meet customer demand
- an inability to reorganise work among existing staff
- an inability to recruit additional staff
- a detrimental impact on quality
- a detrimental impact on performance
- insufficiency of work during the periods the employee proposes to work
- planned structural changes.

 REFLECTIVE ACTIVITY

Two brief summaries of cases that relate to family-friendly employment law are set out below. Read the summaries and then answer the questions that follow.

Edgell v Lloyds Register of Shipping (1977)

Mrs Edgell was employed as a bookkeeper. As part of her job she had the authority to sign cheques up to a specified limit. She also worked without day-to-day supervision, reporting to a senior manager. Following the birth of her child she went on maternity leave. While she was away Lloyds reorganised their bookkeeping division, bringing in new administrative systems and a new organisational structure. When Mrs Edgell returned to work she was given a bookkeeping role at the same grade as she had been on before her leave, but she was no longer able to sign cheques and now worked under a supervisor. She resigned her post and brought two claims to tribunal:

- constructive dismissal
- infringement of the right to return to the same job following maternity leave.

1   Do you think Mrs Edgell should have won either or both of these claims?

British Airways v Moore and Botterill (2000)

Ms Moore and Ms Botterill both worked as air stewardesses on long-haul flights, both becoming pregnant at around the same time. In accordance with the terms of a collective agreement the two women were transferred to ground-based roles once they reached the 16th week of their pregnancies. The intention of the agreement was to ensure that the company complied with its duty to protect the health and safety of pregnant employees. The ground-based jobs were graded at the same level as the in-flight jobs the women carried out and they were equivalent in terms of skills and status. However, because the women were no longer cabin-crew members, they ceased to receive flying allowances in addition to their basic pay. British Airways argued that these allowances did not constitute pay but were intended to cover out-of-pocket expenses incurred by cabin crew members when staying away from home. The women showed that in practice the allowances were more generous, and that they had long considered them to form part of their regular pay packets.

2   Were the women entitled to continue receiving their flying allowances during their pregnancies, even when working in ground-based roles?

MANAGING DISCIPLINE AND POOR PERFORMANCE

A great deal of HR time is taken up with the management of disciplinary matters and of employees who are not performing their jobs to the required standard. We have already discussed some issues in this area, but we now need to focus on it properly. Central here is the law of unfair dismissal. While it is by no means the case that every employee who is guilty of misconduct or poor performance ends up being sacked, managers dealing with such matters always have to have at the back of their minds that the case *might* end up with a dismissal. You therefore always need to handle it from the start in accordance with the expectations of the law. Only then can you be confident that you will be able to defend your actions adequately at an employment tribunal, should that ultimately prove necessary.

Before we look at each main type of situation and at what response the law expects, we must make a few general points about unfair dismissal law.

Firstly, it is important to appreciate that unfair dismissal law only applies to employees. People who work under 'contracts for services' rather than 'contracts of service' cannot bring dismissal claims to an employment tribunal. This includes most casual staff, agency workers and people who are employed on a subcontracted basis. Secondly, for the most part it is only employees who have completed a year's service (two years' if employed after 6 April 2012) who can bring claims. There are significant exceptions to this rule deriving from the presence in the statutes of 'automatically unfair reasons for dismissal' such as pregnancy, trade union membership and refusal to work in unsafe conditions. If one of these is the main reason for a dismissal, the right to bring a claim applies from the first day of employment.

It is also always important to remember that some groups of staff are covered by discrimination laws, which protect them from unlawful dismissals even when the law of unfair dismissal does not. Dismissing someone on the grounds of gender, race or sexual orientation, for example, is always unlawful. And, moreover, all workers and not just employees are covered.

Dismissals on the grounds of misconduct and poor performance are very common. In both case these reasons are classed in law as being 'potentially fair'. This means that an employer has the legal right to dismiss, but must handle the matter in a reasonable fashion. Who wins the case thus hinges on whether or not the employer's actions met the test of reasonableness that has been established in the case law. Above all, this means that the employer must follow the correct procedure. That is why HR managers always 'think legally' from the start when handling these kinds of cases.

ORDINARY MISCONDUCT

Ordinary misconduct is best defined as being a relatively minor breach of an employer's established rules. What exactly comprises a minor breach inevitably varies from workplace to workplace. An airline pilot who had an alcoholic drink prior to flying a plane could not expect his or her employer to treat such a matter as 'ordinary misconduct'. However, if we as university teachers were to have a drink before giving a lecture, it would probably be treated as ordinary misconduct – as long, of course, as we delivered the lecture capably. In most workplaces ordinary misconduct comprises occasional lateness, rudeness to colleagues and minor breaches of health and safety rules.

The response required by the law is:

- conduct a full investigation
- organise a hearing at which the accused employee is able to put his or her case and can be represented by either a work colleague or a trade union representative
- if appropriate, issue a formal warning
- permit an appeal to be made to another/more senior manager.

The key point is that you do not dismiss for a first offence. Instead, a warning is issued, and only if there are subsequent infringements of workplace rules is a lawful dismissal possible.

Some employers have established more complex procedures for dealing with these issues. Sometimes, for example, there is provision for two warnings to be issued before dismissing. Others have policies about the length of time they will hold a warning on file before removing it. None of these is a legal requirement, but as a rule a tribunals expect employers to follow their customary procedures and will find a dismissal to have been unfair if they do not.

GROSS MISCONDUCT

Gross misconduct occurs when an employee breaches an employer's rules in a much more serious way, acting intolerably and destroying trust and confidence in the process. In such circumstances, provided procedures are adhered to, an employer has the right in law to 'summarily dismiss without notice'.

Again, what precisely constitutes gross misconduct in any workplace varies, and employers have a good deal of discretion in deciding for themselves what types of misconduct they will treat as 'gross'. It is important, however, that any rules of this type that are not obvious are communicated effectively. This means that employees know at the time that they breach a rule that they may be dismissed as a result – a situation that makes it much easier to show 'reasonableness' if the matter ever comes to court. Gross misconduct in most workplaces includes fighting, drunkenness, use of illegal drugs, fraud and dishonesty of all kinds. Any employee who does one of these things can expect to be disciplined and summarily dismissed, and should know that their employer has every right to do this.

That said, proper procedures must be followed if a gross misconduct dismissal is to be lawful. As with ordinary misconduct, a full investigation must take place, a hearing convened and a right of appeal provided.

POOR PERFORMANCE

Dismissing people on the grounds of their (lack of) capability is something that most managers hate having to do. It is always a difficult process, particularly in cases of ill health, but it is often necessary for the health of the organisation. The legal principles are actually very straightforward. It is putting them into practice that can be challenging.

In procedural terms, cases of poor performance have to be handled in a very similar way to cases of ordinary misconduct. The procedures used are labelled differently, but the principles are the same. That means that a formal hearing has to be set up at which the employee concerned is warned (again formally) about his or her poor performance. A period of time then has to be agreed during which improvements have to be demonstrated. Ideally, specific performance targets must be set and a programme of training or assistance put in place to help the employee meet them. Performance is then reviewed at a later date and a decision taken at a further hearing about whether or not to dismiss, to issue a further warning, or to let the matter drop. Appeals must also be provided for.

Incapability due to ill health or poor attendance has to be handled in the same way when there is no long-term underlying medical condition. You simply organise a hearing and warn the employee that he or she will be dismissed if attendance does not improve. Again it is best to set clear attendance targets and to give an adequate opportunity for an improvement to occur. It is then lawful to dismiss if these targets are not met.

When someone does have a long-term medical condition that is causing substantial absence, you have to tread much more carefully. In such cases the requirement in law to act reasonably means that the long-term medical prognosis must be taken into account. It would, for example, generally be considered unfair in law to dismiss someone who you knew was recovering and would be likely to return to work in a week or two's time. It is also vital in such cases to take account of disability discrimination law. This applies to anyone who has a serious medical condition (physical or mental) that either has lasted, or could reasonably be expected to last, for 12 months or more. In such cases the employer must not dismiss until it has first gone through a process of considering whether or not there are any reasonable adjustments that could be made that would enable the worker to return to work/continue in the job.

OTHER MAJOR EMPLOYMENT RIGHTS

In the above sections we have summarised and explained many core areas of UK employment regulation. There are, however, several others too. We do not have the space here to go into them in any great detail, so the following paragraphs simply set out the key principles.

HEALTH AND SAFETY LAW

There is a huge body of health and safety law that UK workplaces are obliged to follow, much of it comprising detailed regulations that are of relevance to particular industries. However, there is a single piece of legislation – the Health and Safety at Work Act 1974 – which sets out general principles and places specific obligations on all employers. This Act forms part of the criminal law and is policed by an inspectorate who have considerable powers, including the right to close down an unsafe workplace and to bring criminal prosecutions when serious breaches of the regulations occur. The preamble to the 1974 Act contains the following general statement:

It shall be the duty of every employer to ensure, as far as is reasonably practicable, the health, safety and welfare at work of all his employees.

The Act then goes on to outline the following duties, all of which apply in all workplaces:

- to maintain plant and equipment and to provide safe systems of working
- to ensure safe arrangements for the handling, use, transport and storage of hazardous equipment and/or substances
- to provide all necessary information, training and supervision in the use of hazardous equipment/substances
- to ensure that entrances and exits to buildings are safe and maintained
- to provide adequate facilities and arrangements to ensure welfare at work.

In addition, the Act requires that all workplaces that employ more than five people have in place a written health and safety policy.

Central to health and safety law is the concept of 'risk assessment'. Health and safety inspectors, and indeed the courts, always focus heavily on whether or not these have been carried out. It is far easier for an employer to defend itself if it has done so. Risk assessment simply involves identifying any health and safety hazards and taking appropriate steps to minimise any risks. Such measures must to be written down and the steps followed in practice. In recent years the health and safety inspectorate has shown a particular interest in jobs that are unusually stressful and which leave their holders susceptible to mental breakdown. Risk assessments thus now need to include reference to stressors in the workplace.

PERSONAL INJURY LAW

Stress-related breakdowns also play a major potential role in personal injury law, which is concerned with paying compensation to staff who have suffered serious injury at work. Employees looking to sue their employers in such circumstances have a number of potential avenues to choose from, including resigning and bringing a case of constructive dismissal to an employment tribunal. However, most people – particularly if substantial sums by way of damages are being sought – choose to bring a claim of negligence before the County Court or the High Court.

Most employers in the UK are required by law to have employer's liability insurance, so negligence cases are often more effectively fought by insurance companies seeking to limit their exposure. A number of defences are available for employers to deploy. But by far the most significant is summed up in the following sentence:

The injury was not reasonably foreseeable.

As a result, provided full risk assessments have been carried out and implemented, courts are often obliged to find in favour of the employer. Liability for damages only occurs when an employer knew of a risk and took inadequate steps to deal with it.

BULLYING AND HARASSMENT

Two criminal statutes offer some protection for workers who are bullied by co-workers or by managers at work:

- the Criminal Justice and Public Order Act 1994, which makes it an offence, punishable with up to six months' imprisonment, to cause 'intentional harassment, alarm or distress'
- the Protection from Harassment Act 1997, which is mainly about stalking and situations in which someone places another person in fear of violence. This is also punishable with up to six months' imprisonment.

But in truth neither of these statutes is very helpful to someone being bullied at work. The first requires the prosecution to show that the harasser deliberately sought to harass, alarm or distress, which is difficult to prove and easy to defend. The second requires a genuine fear of physical violence, which is rare in a workplace setting. In extreme cases of bullying these conditions can apply – in which case a report must be made to the police – but most workplace bullying, while distressing, is not in this league.

Much more common are claims made at an employment tribunal accusing a manager or colleague (or more usually a former manager or colleague) of unlawfully harassing. The outcome will be compensation of between £500 and £30,000 if the case is proven, the sum depending on the nature of the harassment suffered and the length of time it was endured.

The problem here, though, is that only a very narrow range of harassment situations qualify and are thus unlawful. The law of harassment forms part of discrimination law, and hence can only cover situations in which detriment is suffered due to one of the protected characteristics listed in the Equality Act 2010 (see above). Nonetheless, this law does offer considerable protection for people who suffer harassment on the grounds, for example, of sex or race.

The primary case is brought against the employer and not the particular harasser. This means that the employer can defend itself by showing that it acted swiftly and appropriately as soon as the complaint was made and that it took all reasonable steps to prevent the harassment from occurring in the first place.

Protection of a more general kind for employees who are bullied at work is provided through the presence in all contracts of employment of a duty on both employers and employees to maintain a relationship of mutual trust and confidence.

Serious bullying is now clearly accepted by the courts, in principle, as constituting a breach on the part of the employer of the duty to maintain a relationship of mutual trust and confidence. And there have been some high-profile cases in this field. The best known is the case of *Horkulak v Cantor Fitzgerald International* (2004), in which a senior manager used threatening and abusive language to a subordinate. Damages were assessed at £900,000 because this was a very highly paid individual.

What does this mean in practice for employers and employees? Firstly, it is possible for an employee or an ex-employee to sue their employer in the County Court or High Court for any financial losses they sustain due to the bullying suffered. There is no need to show that any illness has occurred as a result. Secondly – and much, much more commonly – it makes it possible for an employee who has suffered from being bullied to resign and take a claim of constructive dismissal to an employment tribunal. This latter course of action is much cheaper and is risk-free from the point of view of the employee.

The key test, of course, is what does and what does not constitute bullying. This is a question of judgement – but it must be quite serious for an employee to win a case. In effect, in order to sustain a case, a claimant has to show that the employer acted intolerably and that this led directly to the resignation.

Damages in constructive dismissal cases are generally quite low, and are limited to compensation for financial loss. But employers do not generally relish defending their actions in court, and so the possibility of constructive dismissal proceedings may act as a deterrent and should help to ensure that others are not bullied in the future.

WHISTLEBLOWING

The Public Interest Disclosure Act 1998 gives a measure of protection to 'whistleblowers' who take action when they become concerned about the activities of their employers. Basically, the Act does no more than give whistleblowers protection from victimisation in certain defined circumstances. It covers all workers except those working in the police and security services. Central to the Act is the notion of a 'qualifying disclosure' – that is, one which gives the discloser legal protection. There are five categories named. The disclosure must concern, or be reasonably believed to concern, one of these:

- a criminal offence
- a failure to comply with legal obligations
- a miscarriage of justice (legally, not colloquially, defined)
- compromised health and safety arrangements
- something to cause environmental damage.

Straightforward incompetence or dishonesty are not included, nor is abuse of power unless one of the above is also involved. Moreover, in order to 'qualify', the disclosure must be made in good faith, and only having first exhausted the possibilities for raising the issue with managers internally. Only at this point should representations be made to the authorities.

The whistle can be blown to any of the following:

- the employer
- a legal adviser
- a Minister of the Crown
- appropriate enforcing authorities
- a media organisation.

However, there are restrictions on media disclosures. The qualifying disclosure must relate to 'an exceptionally serious failure' and, moreover, there must be no personal gain.

COLLECTIVE EMPLOYMENT LAW

In the UK, as in most countries, the law gives particular protection to trade unions. The term 'freedom of association' is used in this context to describe the right to join and form trade unions and to participate freely in their activities without any interference from the employer. Importantly, the right of UK employees not to join trade unions is also protected in law. These protections are achieved in three major ways:

- It is considered automatically unfair (and hence unlawful) to dismiss an employee for being a union member, joining a union, taking part in union activities, not being a member, not joining or not taking part in union activities.
- It is also unlawful to subject an employee to 'action short of dismissal' in the same circumstances.
- It is unlawful to discriminate against trade union members when recruiting new staff, or to maintain industry blacklists of union members.

However, once a union and its members engage in any kind of **industrial action**, including strikes, a different set of employment regulations apply, which are a great deal less union-friendly than those which protect freedom of association. As far as union members are concerned, this means that:

- they can lose pay if they fail to perform their contractual duties due to industrial action
- in the case of unofficial industrial action (i.e. wildcat action organised without the knowledge or approval of a union executive committee), employers are free to dismiss at will
- in the case of official action it becomes 'potentially' fair to dismiss after 12 weeks of a dispute.

Union officials who are organising industrial action, as well as unions themselves, are said in law to be 'immune from prosecution in tort' provided they follow set rules about fair balloting, informing the employer about who is going on strike and respecting a seven-day 'cooling-off period' between holding a ballot and the action starting. In practice this means that unions who follow the basic rules on industrial action can never be sued for any damage they may cause to an employer's business by organising it.

Further regulations positively promote union interests. These include measures contained in the Employment Relations Act 1999, which require employers to recognise unions who can demonstrate that they have the support of a good proportion of a workforce, a long-standing right to be consulted on certain types of issue, limitations on how much a union can ever be sued for in court, and the right to represent members in 'serious' disciplinary and grievance proceedings.

👁 Trouble at the big top

All around towns across the country brightly coloured posters proclaim the imminent arrival of Geraldo Pecorino's traditional family travelling circus. Geraldo's round red face smiles out inviting all to gaze and wonder at Alice and Maximilian's amazing feats on the flying trapeze, to gasp in amazement as Little Fat Stan the human cannonball is propelled at speed across the circus ring, to laugh at the crazy antics of Micky the clown and his chums, and to applaud as Daisy the elephant dances daintily on her hind legs. But in reality, Geraldo is not smiling at all. He is very worried about the future of his circus. His star performers may help bring in the crowds, but they are also causing him a variety of managerial headaches.

Alice is his longest-serving artiste. For 35 years, partnered by a succession of male trapeze stars, she has nightly swung and somersaulted high in the air above a safety net, before descending to take her bow. Unfortunately, over time, the once lissom Alice has become less agile and has put on a great deal of weight. As a result, when she enters the ring in her leotard and climbs up to her trapeze the audience increasingly see her as a figure of fun. When she carries out her final triple somersault and falls into the safety net, the structure wobbles alarmingly, causing the audience to scream with laughter. The contrast with the much younger and very athletic Maximilian is becoming more and more obvious, and he is not happy. 'Find me a new partner,' he says, 'or I will find a better circus to work for.' But what can Geraldo do? Alice is well paid and popular among the troupe. For several months he has been able to placate Maximilian by saying that he cannot find a replacement for Alice, but now a perfect new partner for Maximilian has become available. A beautiful 18-year-old

trapeze artist called Melanie who has the rare capacity to carry out a Russian-style backflip quadruple somersault has left a rival circus and is begging Geraldo for a job. Can he sack Alice? Can he redeploy her? Redeployment would be preferable, but the only suitable job he has for her would involve performing with Micky and his crazy clowns. Alice would get the laughs, but it would much be less well-paid work and undignified for a senior artiste with years of loyal service behind her.

Geraldo's second managerial headache concerns another long-serving employee. Jethro has for many years acted as keeper and trainer of Daisy the elephant. They are devoted to one another. Every day Jethro feeds her, cleans her wagon, takes her for walks, washes her and then, in the evening, the two of them perform together to the delight of the audience. For many this act is the highlight of the circus. But six months ago an unfortunate accident occurred. In the middle of their act a large light bulb exploded above the circus ring, which gave Daisy a terrible fright. She panicked and instead of continuing to dance, she charged at Jethro and tossed him into the air. He sustained serious back and neck injuries in this accident and has been in and out of hospital ever since. Geraldo now realises that Jethro will not be able to return to work again for many more months. Daisy is back to her old self and has apparently bonded well with her new keeper, Geraldo's daughter Romola. Jethro visits her when he can, but he comes with his carer and is unable to get up out of his wheelchair. What should Geraldo do? He is still paying Jethro but cannot afford to continue doing so for ever. Can he dismiss him? Should he try to reach a financial settlement, and if so, would his insurance company reimburse him?

And finally, what is Geraldo to do about Little Fat Stan, his much-loved but increasingly awkward human cannonball? Stan has worked in the circus for years, delighting generations of audiences with his acts. He started out as a tumbler. Then as he got older he turned to fire-eating and knife-swallowing, before winding up being fired nightly from a cannon across the ring through several paper hoops and landing spectacularly in a meticulously placed bouncy castle. Stan is not happy. He feels his life is unfulfilled and he wants to change direction. Stan has dealt with his depression in the past by drinking heavily, but has now managed to stop. Instead, he has found great solace by becoming an active Christian. He attends churches in each town that the circus visits and continually regales the other performers with stories about how his faith has changed his life. But this has caused difficulties for Geraldo because Stan has said that he will not in future be available to perform on Sundays or at any time over the Christmas and Easter periods. He has asked Geraldo if he could give up performing and assist him in a management role, taking responsibility for publicising the circus. Failing that he would like to run the box office. But these jobs are already taken and are not, in truth, suitable for Stan. Geraldo insists that he can only employ him as a specialist performer. What should Geraldo do? Mondays and Tuesdays are the days the circus does not put on a performance and on which everyone takes time off. Two performances are mounted every Sunday, and Easter and Christmas are periods when audiences increase substantially. Should he threaten to sack Little Fat Stan? Could he employ someone else to be a human cannonball on Sundays, and reduce Stan's wages to compensate?

The worry of what to do about Stan, Jethro, Maximilian and Alice causes Geraldo to suffer many sleepless nights.

Questions

Geraldo decides that he has no choice but to employ Melanie as a replacement for Alice. He tells Alice that from next week onwards she will have to perform alongside Micky and his clowns. Her role will be to act as his foil and a victim of his many practical jokes. For the next six months she will be paid the same salary that she currently earns. After this date it will be reviewed.

1 Assuming that she is unhappy with Geraldo's decision, what possible legal claims might Alice be able to bring? What defences might Geraldo be able to deploy were Alice to take her case to an employment tribunal?

Geraldo decides to dismiss Jethro, offering him a one-off payment of £25,000 by way of a full and final settlement.

2 What possible legal claims could Jethro bring were he to reject Geraldo's offer? What action could Geraldo take to minimise his chances of losing these cases in court?

Geraldo decides to allow Little Fat Stan to take Sundays off and to take his annual leave over the Christmas and Easter periods. Another performer will be trained up to take his place at these times. In return Geraldo will reduce Stan's pay by 20%.

3 What possible legal claims might Stan be able to bring? How might Geraldo be able to defend himself were the dispute to reach a tribunal hearing?

FURTHER READING

Two books that provide excellent introductions to the key debates about employment law are *Perspectives on Employment Law* by Anne Davies (2009; Cambridge University Press) and *Great Debates in Employment Law* by Simon Honeyball (2011; Palgrave Macmillan).

More general introductions to employment law that have primarily been for people who are not studying law include *Employment Law: An introduction* by Stephen Taylor and Astra Emir (2012; Oxford University Press), and *Essentials of Employment Law* by David Lewis and Malcolm Sargeant (2011; Chartered Institute of Personnel and Development).

REFERENCES

Brewer, N. (2008) Speech at the launch of the 'Working Better' consultation, 14 July. Equal Opportunities Commission.

CIPD (2002) *Employment Law*. Survey report. London, Chartered Institute of Personnel and Development.

CIPD (2012) 'Work audit research', cited in *People Management*, April: 13.

Davies, A. (2009) *Perspectives on Labour Law*, 2nd edition. Cambridge, Cambridge University Press.

Employment Tribunal Service (2011) *Annual Report and Accounts*. London, ETS.

Honeyball, S. (2011) *Great Debates in Employment Law*. Basingstoke, Palgrave Macmillan.

Lea, R. (2001) *Work-Life Balance and All That: The re-regulation of the labour market*. London, Institute of Directors.

Lewis, D. and Sargeant, M. (2011) *Essentials of Employment Law*, 11th edition. London, Chartered Institute of Personnel and Development.

Shackleton, J. R. (2005) 'Regulating the labour market', in P. Booth (ed.) *Towards a Liberal Utopia?* London, Institute of Economic Affairs.

Taylor, S. and Emir, A. (2012) *Employment Law: An introduction*, 3rd edition. Oxford, Oxford University Press.

CHAPTER 3

Resourcing and Talent Planning

Krystal Wilkinson and Stephen Taylor

CHAPTER CONTENTS

- Introduction
- Labour market trends
- Core talent planning
- Developing resourcing strategies
- Managing recruitment and selection
- Maximising employee retention
- Managing retirement, dismissal and redundancy

KEY LEARNING OUTCOMES

By the end of this chapter, you should be able to:

- understand key contemporary labour market trends and their significance for different kinds of organisation and in different contexts

- undertake the various different activities involved in core talent planning

- contribute to the development of organisational resourcing strategies

- design and deliver recruitment and selection activities that are appropriate for the organisation and meet the expectations of the law and good practice

- understand how to maximise employee retention

- appreciate how to manage dismissals, redundancy and retirement effectively and lawfully.

INTRODUCTION

A fundamental part of the human resource (HR) management role is concerned with the mobilisation of a workforce. This means taking responsibility for ensuring that the organisation has the right number of people, with the right skills, at the right time, working in the right places to drive sustained organisation performance. It involves a number of activities including workforce planning, attracting potential employees, selecting the best individuals, retaining employees, succession planning, and managing the departure of staff from the organisation for a number of reasons including retirement, redundancy and dismissal.

Achieving this requires well-considered strategic and operational activity. Organisations are obliged to compete with each other to secure the services of a workforce in labour markets that are continually evolving. One of the major aims of this chapter is thus to introduce the reader to the strategic approaches that organisations take to position themselves as employers in the labour market and plan effectively so that they are able to meet their current and anticipated organisational skills needs. Another is to introduce the operational tools, techniques and practices that organisations need to use to resource their organisations.

LABOUR MARKET TRENDS

The term **'labour market'** is a key concept in employee resourcing. The traditional definition of a market is 'an actual or nominal place where forces of demand and supply operate, and where buyers and sellers interact (directly or through intermediaries) to trade' (www.businessdictionary.com). Thus in marketing, organisations are concerned with the market(s) for their products or services – identifying which people or companies might be willing and able to purchase, and determining what these groups are looking for. A labour market concerns the market for potential employees – which people may be willing and able to work for the company, and what they are looking for in terms of employment.

SOURCES OF LABOUR

There are a number of different sources of potential employees in the overall labour market. Sources of labour include:

- job-seekers in the local market
  These are people who are actively looking for employment and to live in the local area. They are especially useful where companies are looking to fill low-skill roles.
- job-seekers in the national market
  These are people who are actively looking for employment anywhere in the country. They tend to be more suited to companies that are looking to fill skilled/specialist roles – where salaries are likely to be higher, and individuals are willing to relocate for the right job.
- job-seekers in the international market
  These are people who are actively looking for employment anywhere in the world. These tend to be more appropriate again for higher-skilled specialist or shortage roles, especially following the changes in immigration laws that have made it harder for job-seekers to enter the UK.
- individuals working in other companies

These are people who are not actively looking for employment but who may well have the skills and experience that another company wants. They may be interested in changing employer if the right package is offered.

- graduates
  These are people who are highly educated, who are actively looking for employment, and who often want some form of structured development plan.
- school- or college-leavers
  These are people who are new to the world of work. They are actively looking for employment but might require more investment from an organisation in terms of training and development.
- the economically inactive
  These are people who are not currently either in employment or looking for employment, but who could enter the workforce if the appropriate incentives or provisions were made available. The group includes people who have retired, people with long-term health problems, and those with childcare or eldercare commitments. More attention has been paid to this group, and how they can be brought into the workforce, over the last decade or so – as competition for workers has increased.

It is important to be aware that different companies therefore focus on different labour markets when coming up with their recruitment strategies – something we discuss further later on.

TIGHT AND LOOSE MARKETS

When considering a labour market, one of the main things to understand is that the ease with which organisations can recruit employees depends on the nature of the market they are targeting at that specific point in time – whether it is 'tight' or 'loose'.

A **tight labour market** refers to a situation in which there are more job opportunities available than there are active job-seekers, meaning that companies find it more difficult to fill their vacancies because job-seekers have a considerable degree of choice. A **loose labour market** therefore refers to the opposite situation – in which there are many job-seekers competing for a smaller number of opportunities.

When markets are tight, employers are required to be more creative with their people management recruitment strategies, often focusing on the following:

- employer branding
  We cover this in more detail later, but the term basically refers to activities designed to formulate a specific (and attractive) personality for the company, and to promote it to potential employees.
- recruitment initiatives
  Investing money in innovative recruitment techniques, targeting a broader pool of potential applicants.
- retention strategies
  Investigating the reasons for departures from the company, and finding ways to tackle those that suggest or constitute a problem.

- reorganisations
  Changing the way that job tasks are allocated in order to minimise the need for hard-to-recruit staff. A 'skill-mix review' can be carried out to ensure that the people who are the hardest to recruit (usually with specific skills) can spend all of their time on the tasks that only they can complete, and that other things are delegated to others.
- development initiatives
  Enhancing the skills of the current workforce, and bringing in people who do not have the required skills yet but who are interested in developing them.
- long-term resource planning
  The company could collaborate with local universities or training providers to increase the number of people with the relevant skills in the future.

 REFLECTIVE ACTIVITY

Suppose the NHS were to find itself in a situation where it was proving very difficult to locate surgeons with the knowledge and experience required to perform a specific type of heart surgery. Bearing the above list in mind, how might the organisation best tackle the problem?

TRENDS IN THE DEMAND AND SUPPLY OF SKILLS

Over time, the national labour market and specific parts of it (different regions and industries) can be seen to expand (loosen) and contract (tighten) owing to a range of factors. These include:

- the economic context
  An economic downturn usually has a significant effect on the labour market, because many companies will be forced to close or to downsize, resulting in either case in staff redundancies.
- demographic changes
  The number of births and deaths, etc.
- political changes
  Things like immigration policies and investment in national skills development have an effect on the number of people in the labour market and their usefulness to employing organisations.
- legislative changes
  Employment laws limiting working hours can increase the demand for numbers of employees, and legislation concerning non-discrimination can open up the labour market to groups traditionally excluded (e.g. those who are disabled or past retirement age).
- technological developments
  Advancements in automation can make a lot of workers superfluous in certain industries while at the same time increasing the demand for those with technical expertise.
- natural disasters or international events (such as war)

These can wipe out or divert a considerable proportion of the labour force. At a local level, the introduction or removal of competitors can have an impact.

Over the last few years, the UK labour market in general has been loosening. Although the main reason for this has been the economic downturn, a number of other factors can also be considered, such as the fairly open immigration policies of recent years, increased international competition, jobs being exported to cheaper countries, and the development of labour-saving technologies. In such a loose labour market, organisations often pay little attention to employee recruitment and retention – because employees are unlikely to voluntarily leave a job.

Having said this, in relation to longer-term trends the picture is somewhat different. Over the past few decades, the main trend has been for increasing levels of employment. When data on the number of jobs in the UK was first recorded in 1960, the figure stood at 26.1 million. In the 50 years that followed, this figure grew to 31.4 million. The increase has not been consistent year on year. The number of jobs grew particularly steeply in the mid-1980s (in a time of general growth and prosperity), but importantly, also dipped a few times during these decades – during periods of recession. When such dips occurred in the past, they were followed not only by recovery but by a continuance of the general pattern of growth. Based on this information, we can speculate that the labour market may well start tightening again moving forward.

So would this be a problem? During the past 50 years, the ongoing increase in the number of jobs available has not been problematic because the number of people seeking employment has also been rising – a result of three social and demographic trends:

- a steady increase in the number of women entering the workforce
- the 'baby-boom' generation (which refers to the large cohort of individuals born in the years following the end of the Second World War) being of working age
- increasing numbers of immigrants entering the UK for work.

Assuming that the economy picks up again after the current recession, and the long-term trend for increasing jobs resumes, where does this leave us in terms of the ability of supply to meet demand? Worryingly, all three of the trends cited above are unlikely to continue – meaning that labour markets are likely to tighten considerably – and organisations and their HR teams will need to respond.

SOCIAL AND DEMOGRAPHIC TRENDS

The two main demographic factors that affect the labour market are the age-profile of the population, and trends surrounding immigration. It is widely known that the UK, alongside most countries in Europe, has an ageing population. In the decades since the 'baby boom' of the 1960s there has been an ongoing reduction in the number of children being born each year. When combined with the trend for young people to stay in full-time education for longer than they used to, it means that considerably fewer young people are entering the labour market each year than they did in the past.

This becomes a significant problem when we combine it with the fact that many of the 'baby-boom' generation are approaching retirement age – which means a considerable loss of skilled workers from the labour market at the other end of the cycle. The government has introduced a range of provisions to encourage older workers to remain in employment for longer, such as the removal of the default retirement age and the introduction of employment protection from discrimination on the grounds of age, but this is unlikely to be enough to stop the volume of the working-age population reducing year on year.

In terms of immigration levels, the trend for the last 50 years has been a steady increase in the percentage of the UK population that was born overseas – from around 4% in 1951 to over 8% in 2001. This is unlikely to continue, however, because the UK population as a whole has been growing at a rate that is not economically sustainable (in terms of housing, transport and public service provision). One way that the government has responded is to tighten immigration policies – so that only migrants who have specific skills (that are in short supply in the home market) are permitted to enter the country and live here.

GOVERNMENT AND STATE SKILLS STRATEGIES

Given the concerns about a discrepancy between the nature of the skills needed by UK employers and the level of skills available in the working-age population, and the failure of the UK to compete on a global scale owing to skills levels, the former government put in place a wide-ranging and formal skills review in 2004. Led by the Chairman of the National Employment Panel, Sandy Leitch, the final report was published in 2006, detailing two key areas for action: improving levels of basic skills, and improving levels of higher-level specialist, professional and technical skills.

'Basic skills' refers to basic literacy and numeracy. In response to this part of the Leitch Report, the government published the *World-Class Skills* White Paper, which set some ambitious targets for skills levels to be reached by 2020. Targets included having 95% of adults functionally literate and numerate (currently 85% and 79% respectively); over 90% of adults having gained a Level-2 qualification – GCSE or equivalent (currently 69%); and having 500,000 people on apprenticeship schemes. In support of such targets, the government set in motion an increase in the education-leaving age (this will be 18 years from 2015), and has focused on collaboration with educational providers and employers.

In terms of improving higher-level specialist, professional and technical skills, the focus of the government has been on 'turning the old system on its head', so that training and development provision are demand-led (determined by the needs of business) rather than via bureaucratic central planning and regulatory control. The strategy is summarised in the 2010 Department for Business, Innovation and Skills strategy document entitled *Skills For Sustainable Growth*.

LABOUR MARKET FLEXIBILITY AND THE IMPORTANCE OF FLEXIBLE WORKING

In addition to improving overall skills levels in the UK, another way to maximise the potential of the labour market is to ensure that organisations are as flexible as possible. Flexibility is actually one of the key emerging issues for organisations of the twenty-first century, closely associated with the rate of change in the wider environment and the requirement for organisations to be able to adapt to such changes quickly. The terms 'labour market flexibility' and 'flexible working' are associated with a considerable number of strategies that companies can use to get maximum value out of the individuals working for them.

One of the leading authors in the field is John Atkinson (1984a), who noted four types of flexibility strategy used by modern companies:

- external numerical flexibility
  This involves the company having the ability to increase or decrease the total headcount of the organisation based on peaks and troughs in demand. It is usually achieved by supplementing a minimal permanent workforce with a periphery group of workers on various forms of 'atypical' contract (including temporary contracts, fixed-term contracts, seasonal contracts and 'zero-hour'/ casual contracts).
- internal numerical flexibility
  Sometimes referred to as 'temporal flexibility' or 'working time flexibility', this involves the company adjusting the working hours or schedules of the people already employed in the firm. It therefore includes part-time, flexi-time, flexible working hours/shifts (including nights, weekend shifts, split shifts) and overtime. One of the main benefits to the business is the ability to cater for the 24/7 nature of much modern business without needing to employ more people. A number of people on different, relatively short shifts can often provide more effective cover than a smaller group of full-time staff, but the wage cost is the same.
- functional flexibility
  This involves the company increasing the extent to which employees can be transferred to different activities and tasks within the firm. It has to do with the organisation of operations (job rotation) and the training of workers (multi-skilling), and enables the company to allocate staff to where they are most needed on a day-to-day basis.
- financial or wage flexibility
  This refers to a system in which pay levels are not decided collectively, so that employment costs can reflect the supply and demand of labour. It can be achieved by rate-for-the-job systems or an assessment-based pay system, or individual performance wages.

Although the primary aim of flexibility strategies is to make the organisation more responsive and they are therefore said to be 'employer-friendly', it should be noted that some of the strategies are also said to be 'employee-friendly'.

In a different publication, Atkinson (1984b) described the ultimate 'flexible firm', which combines different types of flexibility in a core/periphery model:

The organisation employs a relatively small 'core' workforce, which consists of permanent full-time employees, who are trained to be functionally flexible and are responsible for carrying out the company's key firm-specific competencies. Because the organisation wants to develop long-term relationships with these individuals, they are offered considerable reward and employment security.

In order to protect the employment of this core workforce, the company then makes use of a 'periphery' workforce that acts as a buffer to the core group – in that they can be easily up- or downsized as required. Rather than functional flexibility, the key strategies employed for this group are internal and external numerical flexibility.

CORE TALENT PLANNING

Now that we have examined the idea of labour markets and different sources of potential employees, we can move on to the issue of talent planning. Sometimes described as 'human resource planning' (HRP), this refers to the activities carried out by a company to consider the specific employees and skills that it will need in the future, and to put in place strategies to ensure that it can meet these requirements – which may well involve turning to the labour market for more people. It involves ensuring that the company will have 'the right people, with the right skills, in the right places at the right time' to fulfil the company's strategic objectives.

Talent planning can vary in terms of both scope (one department, one site, national or international) and time-scale (are we thinking next year or ten years' time?). There are, however, four stages that should be followed:

- forecasting the company's future demand for skills
- forecasting what skills the company will have in the future
- identifying any gap between the future demand and supply of skills
- making plans to fill any gap.

FORECASTING DEMAND

Forecasting the demands that the company will have for skills in the future is the first stage of the talent planning process. It involves asking the following questions:

- What tasks will need doing?
- How can these best be divided into individual job roles? We need to consider the type of role (part-time, full-time, contract) as well as numbers.
- What skills are needed for each role?

So how do we get started in answering these questions? How can we know what our requirement will be in the future? There are a number of approaches that can be taken:

- *systematic techniques*, which can include things like a) looking at past trends to predict future needs; and b) working back from the outputs desired
- *managerial judgement*, which is based on the knowledge and experience of senior staff of the specific company, the industry and the external environment
- *working back from costs*, which begins with the future budget and then determines how many staff can be afforded.

From such activities we should be able to identify roughly what job roles are needed, how many people are needed in each and what skills are needed. From this we can draw up specific job descriptions and person specifications (covered below).

FORECASTING SUPPLY

When we know how many people we need, and with what skills, the next thing we must do is look at the current resources of the company. We must consider the composition of the current workforce, the skills of this workforce and the proportion of this workforce that is likely to remain at the time that we are forecasting for.

In terms of understanding the current workforce, we need to get to identify the total number of people employed, the total wage cost, the workforce composition (percentages employed in each department, at each grade, in different age groups and with different lengths of service) and the levels of sickness absence (and the impact this has on the ability to deliver services).

After looking at the people that we currently have, we must assess the skills they have, which can be done by consulting person specifications for current job roles (more on this later), appraisal information and internal training records.

Finally, we must estimate the number of these employees that are likely to still be employed in the future. The most important thing to think about here is general trends in employee turnover – how many people tend to resign each year, how many people are approaching retirement age? More sophisticated analyses will also consider the roles that people will be working in, considering the number of lateral moves and promotions that are likely as well.

IDENTIFYING GAPS BETWEEN DEMAND AND SUPPLY

Once we have information on the job roles and skills that we will need in the future, and on the job roles and skills we have in the present, we can conduct a skills audit for the majority of the common roles in order to determine the extent of the mismatch between the two. Put simply, there are three steps to this activity:

1   Create a competency framework for each of the common roles. This would be a list of all of the competencies (desirable human characteristics) that are required for the role, and an indication of the level of skill required. An example for a call centre operative might be:

2   Assess each current employee using an audit form. Each individual's line manager is best placed to complete the audit, and should base assessments on personal judgement, observation and discussion with the individual (including scenario-based questions on how they would handle a situation).

3   Summarise the results for the whole workforce to identify the total skills currently available, and the extent to which this matches the skills base needed for the future.

ADDRESSING THE GAPS

There are two main areas that must be considered next. The first is to determine how the company can best use its existing resources. This might involve moving people, training people (in the current or in a different area), encouraging knowledge-sharing (coaching and mentoring), ensuring the retention of valued people (discussed below), and removing some individuals if their skills and aspirations unfortunately do not match future needs (discussed below).

The second is to identify what external sources of skills can be utilised. This involves assessing the nature of the local labour market, contemplating recruitment from further afield, and considering the usefulness of bringing people in on a contract basis or collaborating with other organisations (charities/universities, etc) in relation to work experience programmes. Another angle is to consider the value of outsourcing or off-shoring certain activities. The former refers to securing an external provider for an activity rather than doing it in-house, and the latter to securing a foreign provider.

SUCCESSION PLANNING

One activity that is often cited interchangeably with talent planning – but which actually refers to a distinct activity – is succession planning. Whereas talent planning refers to overall staffing considerations, succession planning refers to a group of activities that aim to ensure that at any time an organisation has sufficient numbers of people with the ability, knowledge, personal attributes and experience necessary to step into roles at the next level when they become vacant.

The original focus of succession planning was at the very highest levels of a company – to ensure a smooth transition when a director or a very senior manager departs, and to avoid having to react quickly and ask someone to 'act up' for a temporary period, to promote someone who is not prepared or to recruit someone from outside the organisation who doesn't know the company and the way things are done. The process therefore concerned the selection and grooming of a chosen few. It has since been extended to cover the whole workforce, however. Rather than targeting specific individuals for specific roles, the aim is to develop 'pools of talent' from which a replacement can be selected as and when a vacancy becomes available.

Appraisal meetings are central to the process – identifying the aspirations of employees, assessing current skills levels and agreeing development plans moving forward. A range of development activities can be utilised to help furnish individuals with the skills they will need at the next level, including formal training programmes, on-the-job training and coaching, work shadowing, mentoring schemes, experience in different departments, supervised 'acting up', and things like attendance at committees and ownership of special projects.

One long-standing debate in the field of HR planning is how to balance succession planning with a desire for 'new blood' – bringing in people from outside the business who may have fresh ideas and perspectives. The CIPD factsheet (CIPD, 2012a) suggests that companies should aim for a ratio of around 80:20 between insiders and outsiders, and should avoid appointing outsiders at board level, where an awareness of corporate culture is key.

FAIR ACCESS TO OPPORTUNITY

When considering activities in the field of talent planning (deployment, development and career management), it is essential that companies give all employees fair access to the opportunities available. There are several ways to help ensure this:

- extensive communication of opportunities to all
- mechanisms whereby anyone can express an interest in opportunities
- fairness in selection – open competition for opportunities and formal selection criteria (as opposed to management discretion)
- regular appraisals for all employees – with development goals to help them move towards longer-term aspirations
- positive action initiatives: forms of assistance for those who may be disadvantaged in some respect. For example, if women are under-represented at management level in a company, a management skills course targeted at female staff might be developed
- auditing of training records and/or the inclusion of training and development questions in any employee satisfaction surveys
- making a variety of development provisions available so that all employees are catered for – including those with different learning styles, those with atypical working patterns and those at different stages of their careers
- in the case of redeployment, making certain that all individuals involved are fully consulted
- working with all management staff on the importance of equality of opportunity and on career management in general. It is important that managers are not, for example, blocking the development of a promising

subordinate for fear that the individual might move to another department or even take over their own job.

DEVELOPING RESOURCING STRATEGIES

When an organisation is faced with the task of developing a targeted resourcing strategy, it must be aware that it is not operating in isolation. To be successful, the resourcing strategy of an organisation should be based on attracting the right people, and differentiating the company from the competition. In this brief section of the chapter three key activities are examined: competitor analysis, organisation positioning in relation to the labour market, and **employer branding.**

COMPETITOR ANALYSIS

Before any decisions are taken in relation to the optimum resourcing strategy for the organisation, it is important to be aware of what competitors are doing. 'Competitors' here refers to labour market competitors, which are not necessarily the same as product market competitors. If, for example, your organisation is a food-processing factory and you need to recruit a number of low-skill local workers, the companies that you should consider are not necessarily the dominant food-processing companies in the UK but rather the other companies in the local area that employ low-skill workers (shops, restaurants, other factories, etc).

When conducting an analysis, you need to think of both the strengths and the weaknesses of the employment deal offered by each competitor – which includes things like the salary offered, other benefits, employment security, job role, working environment, and opportunities for training and development.

Once you are aware of what the competition is offering, you are in a better place to consider what you can offer to potential employees that may make your company stand out from the crowd.

ORGANISATION POSITIONING

Although it is up to the individual organisation to decide how it would like to present itself to the labour market, it has been noted that there are some common overall approaches. Taylor (2011) cites the following useful typology offered by Higgs (2004):

The approaches are differentiated based on two factors: *reward* (the amount of money the employer is willing or able to pay its employees) and *culture* (the extent to which employees are respected and treated ethically).

An 'employer of cash' tends to treat employees quite harshly, perhaps autocratically or expecting them to work excessive hours, but compensates them by paying them well.

An 'employer of values' is the polar opposite – it often cannot afford to pay people the going market rate but is committed to treating employees very well (offering fair treatment, rewarding work, job security). The approach tends to be associated with the public and voluntary sectors.

An 'employer of churn' tends to both pay poorly and treat employees harshly. The result is often high staff turnover levels, which means that such an approach is only a viable possibility in loose labour market conditions – when staff can be easily replaced. Target groups are often those with low skill levels (and with little choice of alternative employment), workers recruited from overseas and students looking for temporary work.

To be an 'employer of choice' is perceived to be the optimal strategic aim, especially where labour markets are tight, and involves both paying well and treating people positively. Companies with this approach tend to make it on to the annual *Sunday Times* list of the '100 best companies to work for'.

EMPLOYER BRANDING

Employer branding is about presenting your organisation to the labour market in the best possible light so that potential employees would like to work for you more than your competitors. The CIPD's definition of an employer brand is:

> a set of attributes and qualities, often intangible, that makes an organisation distinctive, promises a particular kind of employment experience, and appeals to those people who will thrive and perform best in its culture.

It is based on the principles of product branding and advertising developed in marketing.

There has been a lot of interest in employee branding in recent years, and a degree of consensus has emerged on how organisations should go about it. The most important thing appears to be that the brand message that is developed *must* reflect the reality of working for the company. If the employer markets itself by making false claims, all that will follow is that any new recruits will be disappointed, current employees will be confused and cynical, and gradually the reputation of the organisation will suffer. To ensure that the brand reflects the reality, the starting point of any activity in this area should be research into the perceptions of existing members of staff. The key things to discover are what aspects of the employment experience are perceived to be both positive and unique (different from that of other employers).

There are some useful frameworks available for managers to consult when deciding how best to present themselves to potential employees. The idea is that there are different 'personalities' that organisations can align themselves with. Lievens *et al* (2007), for example, offer the following five options:

- sincerity – branding based on being honest and friendly
- excitement – branding based on being trendy, spirited and innovative. An example is Google, who market the following on their website:

> In every Google office, you will find challenging projects and smart people with potential to change the world. Googlers relish the freedom to

create the next generation of web technologies in an environment designed to foster collaboration, creativity, health, and happiness.

- competence – branding based on being reliable and successful
- sophistication – branding based on being prestigious
- ruggedness – branding based on being masculine and tough.

Once the analysis is complete and the key factors that differentiate the employment experience have been clearly established, the next step is to develop slogans and statements that can be used to communicate the key messages to existing and to would-be staff. A feature of employer branding is the need to repeat the core message again and again and again over a prolonged period using every available opportunity.

Transforming an employer brand

CASE STUDY

McDonald's is truly a global brand – being one of the largest and most successful food chains in the world, operating over 31,000 outlets spread across 119 countries. It would be almost impossible to dispute the success of the McDonald's corporate brand – but what about the employer brand?

Traditionally, McDonald's has had a poor reputation as an employer. This derives from the cost leadership strategy employed, most jobs being of the entry-level, low-skill, low-autonomy variety, and relatively poorly paid. Although McDonald's has by no means been alone in offering this type of employment, its sheer prevalence made it a commonly cited example – leading to the unfortunate term 'McJob' appearing at the end of the 1990s, being used in connection with any low-prestige, low-benefit, no-future type of employment, usually in the service sector.

Aware of the damage such a reputation would do – to both the morale of the existing workforce and efforts to attract new employees – McDonald's has been working hard to systematically redefine the 'McJob' term and improve its employer brand image since. It has done this by continually working on the benefits it offers to employees, and ensuring that these are well promoted. The current employee benefit portfolio includes a range of work–life balance provisions, a range of recognition programmes, and impressive training and development provision, including its own corporate 'Hamburger University'.

REFLECTIVE ACTIVITY

What would you say was the employer brand of your own organisation (or an organisation that you are familiar with)?

MANAGING RECRUITMENT AND SELECTION

Recruitment and **selection** tend to be lumped together as contributory parts of a process of bringing new employees into a company. It is important to be aware, however, that the terms refer to two different sets of activities. 'Recruitment' refers to advertising the company and the vacancy to potential employees, and trying to encourage suitable individuals to apply, whereas 'selection' refers to choosing the most suitable candidate from those who have applied.

MANAGING THE RECRUITMENT PROCESS

Recruitment is a required activity in two different circumstances: when a new job role is created within a business, and when an existing employee leaves the business. Before any recruitment activities commence, however, it is important that thorough consideration is given first to determining that a vacancy has definitely arisen (and that the job tasks cannot be distributed among existing employees), and second, if a vacancy has arisen, to knowing exactly what skills and experience are needed to fill it.

In order to determine the skills and experiences needed for a role, some form of job analysis is generally undertaken, which collects information from a range of sources on job duties, job responsibilities, the equipment, tools and materials used, controls over work, interactions with others, performance expectations, the working environment, and any prerequisites in terms of education/experience.

The range of sources from which such information can come is wide. If the role is not a new one, information on it can come from current role-holders (via observation of them at work, via interviews or via the completion of work diaries). Information can also be collected from the line manager for the role, from other organisation stakeholders who would have contact with the individual, from documentary evidence such as appraisal results and training manuals, and from external experts in the specific field.

After the job analysis, the steps described below are commonly followed.

Developing a job description

The job description is one of the key documents in recruitment and selection activities. Based on the job analysis exercise, it summarises the tasks that make up the job, together with statements of reporting lines, areas of responsibility and performance criteria. IRS (2003: 43) found that over 75% of employers include copies of job descriptions in application packs, and that 82% use them when drawing up job advertisements.

Job descriptions tend to follow a standard format from company to company, usually listing the following information:

- job title
- grade/rate of pay
- main location
- supervisor's name/post

- details of any subordinates
- summary of the main purpose of the job
- list of principal job duties together with very brief descriptions
- reference to other documents (such as collective agreements) that may clarify or expand on other items.

Developing a person specification

Whereas the job description focuses on the nature of the role, the accompanying person specification focuses on the human attributes that are considered to be necessary for someone performing the role. IRS (2003) found that 72% of employers make use of person specifications. Person specifications tend to include information under a number of headings, including:

- skills – such as a certain level of IT competence, a foreign language, familiarity with certain tools and techniques
- experience – in a similar job role, company or industry
- qualifications – generally vocational
- education – mostly referring to a specific level (i.e. GCSEs, A-level or degree)
- personal attributes – such as professionalism, creativity, interpersonal skills.

It is also typical for each specification to be classified as either 'essential' or 'desirable' in the person performing the role.

Identifying useful sources

The most appropriate source for filling a vacancy will depend on the nature of the job. Companies can look to individuals currently working in the company (who may be interested in a promotion or even a sideways move) as well as those in the outside labour market.

Identifying the most appropriate advertising methods

There is a huge range of options available, including:

- internal company methods (staff intranet, notice-boards)
- word of mouth – encouraging current employees to recommend the company to others who may be suitable ('refer-a-friend' schemes)
- a variety of print advertisements (local newspapers, national newspapers, specialist trade magazines)
- online advertisements
- local radio
- job centres
- employment agencies
- educational liaison – careers service, career fairs, college tutors, student societies.

Along with the suitability of different methods for reaching the required labour market, the costs of the different options are likely to be key considerations.

MANAGING THE SELECTION PROCESS

Once the fruits of a successful recruitment campaign have appeared, and a company has a number of eager individuals expressing an interest in the job(s) available, the next task for the company is to identify which individuals are best suited to both the job(s) and the culture of the company.

The first task at this stage is often the development of a competency framework to use throughout the selection process (generally produced at the same time as the job description and person specification). This document was mentioned earlier in connection with the skills audit activity in talent planning. Because companies tend to place great emphasis on their 'core values', and want these to permeate throughout the business, many organisations have a fixed list of competencies (linked to the core values) against which all jobs are assessed. It has been noted that the most commonly sought competencies in UK organisations include communication, customer focus, commercial awareness, teamwork, flexibility and problem-solving.

To assess each applicant against the requirements of the competency framework for the role, a number of selection techniques can be used. The major methods are:

Application procedures

Such procedures mostly focus on the instructions given to those interested in the vacancies in terms of registering their interest (usually by submitting a CV or completing the company's standard application form), together with subsequent in-house procedures for sifting through the pile of applications to identify the most promising – a process of short-listing.

Interviews

A range of options is available:

- telephone interviews
  These tend to be common as a first stage in the process, to identify those suitable for a more substantial interview, or where candidates are being recruited from overseas.
- face-to-face, one-to-one interviews
  These are usually conducted by a member of the HR department or by the line manager of the vacant role.
- panel interviews
  This is where more than one company representative attends the interview.
- group interviews
  This approach differs in that it involves a group of applicants being interviewed at the same time by a recruitment team. Sometimes tasks may be set which the interviewers observe, such as one candidate interviewing another.

There is no one set format for any of these types of interview, and the nature can vary considerably from company to company. In the past, interviews tended to be fairly unstructured, different candidates being asked different questions based on the factors cited on their CVs/application forms. Given the concerns about consistency in treatment, however, interviews tend to be more structured these days, the interviewers following a fixed interview schedule but then tailoring the discussion to the specific interviewee when probing and seeking examples.

In line with the popularity of competencies in the workplace cited above, many companies now use competency-based interviewing, where applicants are asked to provide examples of how they have demonstrated a certain competency in the past, or answer a scenario-based question that aims to draw out how they would act in a specific circumstance.

Ability and personality tests

According to the CIPD's 2009 Recruitment, Retention and Turnover survey, around half of the UK's larger employers now use some form of ability testing when selecting at least some of their employees. There are different types of tests, including those measuring general ability (such as IQ tests), those measuring literacy and/or numeracy, and those measuring skills in job-specific activities. It is important to be aware that these tests are never used in isolation – their primary purpose is to weed out the poorest performers in short-listing from huge numbers of applicants (such as in highly competitive graduate recruitment schemes) and to provide supplementary information for consideration alongside the data from other selection techniques.

Along with ability tests, a range of personality tests is also available for use in employee selection (as well as employee development). According to the CIPD's 2009 survey, they are used to some extent by 35% of UK organisations, and are especially common when considering management and trainee management roles – where softer, less tangible skills such as communication, diplomacy and emotional intelligence are often deemed necessary. The tests usually consist of personality questionnaires or inventories that candidates complete either on paper or online. Unlike ability tests, there are no 'correct' answers to questions, but the outcomes are used to determine the extent to which each candidate's natural personality matches the disposition deemed to be most suited to the specific position.

Work samples and assessment centres

Work samples are required when organisations ask candidates to complete some element of the job role as part of the selection procedure to demonstrate their competence.

Assessment centres are perhaps the most sophisticated of all the available selection activities: they are designed to bring together a group of applicants and assess each individual using a range of different selection methods. Assessment centres often include a combination of two or more of the following:

- candidate presentations
- interviews
- individual work samples (such as in-tray exercises)
- ability and/or personality tests

- group activities
- role-playing.

The advantage of the method is that it offers a much more valid measure of each individual's suitability for the role (cross-referencing the results of different information sources). The disadvantages of the method are that it is only viable where there are a reasonably large number of candidates, and that it tends to be very costly.

References

Regardless of the specific selection methods used by a company, once the preferred candidate has been identified, most companies seek to further check the suitability of the candidate by securing references. A reference is a testimonial from someone who knows the candidate well, which comments on the candidate's suitability for employment. It is common practice for a company to request two references prior to making or confirming an offer of employment to a candidate – either both from previous employers (or educational contacts if they are new to the world of work), or one professional and one personal.

In the past, companies would ask for quite a lot of information about candidates when making reference requests. But with fears of backlash from disgruntled ex-employees (including threats of legal action), however, employers have become far more reluctant when it comes to providing information in response to reference requests, especially anything that is subjective (personal opinion on performance/attitude, etc). A common approach these days is therefore to provide simply the job title, dates of employment and overall reason for leaving (whether resignation, retirement, redundancy or dismissal).

KEY LEGAL REQUIREMENTS IN RECRUITMENT AND SELECTION

Under the Equality Act 2010, all employers have a legal responsibility to ensure that no unlawful discrimination occurs in the recruitment and selection process on the grounds of what is known as a 'protected characteristic'. This covers sex, race, nationality, disability, age, marital status, sexual orientation, and religion or belief. Unlawful discrimination can be direct, indirect or even 'positive'. It is also important to be aware that there are additional requirements to consider in relation to applicants with a disability. More details on this subject can be found in Chapter 2, *Employment Law*.

There are also legal requirements to consider in the induction of new employees once selected, such as checking their eligibility to work in the UK, and ensuring that they are issued with an employment contract (a written statement of the main terms of employment) within two months of starting work.

Diversity and fair access to opportunities

As stated above, it is a legal requirement that organisations do not make any negative decisions about employment based on a protected characteristic. In order to ensure fair access to opportunity in recruitment and selection, however, organisations should go further than simply ensuring that personal factors do not influence the selection decision. They should also take steps to ensure that all individuals have an equal opportunity to apply. To ensure fair access to opportunity, the following can be considered:

- advertising vacancies via a range of different mechanisms to target a diverse population
- auditing the diversity of the workforce, and making use of positive action campaigns if a certain group is found to be under-represented
- offering alternative options for application – for example, large-print versions of application forms; online and paper submission options – and ensuring that the HR department contact details are clearly displayed for those who would like to discuss their specific circumstances
- offering provisions at the selection stage – for example, allowing candidates to bring a support worker to an interview or to be given more time in tests if they are disabled; people might otherwise be offered a telephone rather than a face-to-face interview if they are based overseas.

THE EVALUATION OF PRACTICES

The final thing to consider before we move on from recruitment and selection is the importance of evaluation. For a start, it is important to ensure that the tools and processes used are proving effective – attracting and identifying the best people for the jobs available. Equally important is to be able to prove that the activities are cost-effective. In the modern business environment, all functions – including human resources – are under increasing pressure to demonstrate to the senior management team how they add value to the business. Employee resourcing can be one of the HR team's most costly activities, and so it is essential that the benefits are seen to outweigh the costs.

So how can we evaluate our recruitment and selection practices?

- By monitoring the statistics – such as the average length of time that vacancies are live, the overall number of applications (are we attracting people?), the percentage of applicants initially short-listed (are we attracting the right people?), and the percentage of offers accepted.
- By recording the costs of recruitment and selection activities and seeing how they compare to previous years' costs (internal benchmarking) or to the costs of other companies in the industry (external benchmarking).
- By monitoring turnover levels – especially in the first few months of employment.
- By holding focus groups with a group of new starters during the induction process.

MAXIMISING EMPLOYEE RETENTION

As well as understanding how to bring the right people into the company to fill vacancies, it is essential that the employee resourcing team are competent in maximising employee retention – ensuring that the right people don't leave the company and create more vacancies that need filling.

There are two general approaches that can be taken – usually in tandem – when considering how to maximise employee retention: one looking outside the organisation (considering trends in the labour market and what your competitors are doing) and the other looking inside the organisation (at your current turnover levels and the reasons for voluntary departures).

We focus on the latter here – understanding the current turnover situation in the company. It is important to understand that not all turnover is bad. A certain amount of turnover, sometimes termed 'functional turnover', is desired because it concerns things like the removal of poor performers, savings on wages and facilitating the progression of other employees and the entry of 'new blood' into the organisation.

That said, a lot of employee turnover falls under the heading of 'dysfunctional turnover' – staff departures that have a negative effect on the company, seen in terms of the significant costs involved in replacing employees, the loss of skills and knowledge, etc, and the negative effect on remaining colleagues.

In order to understand the turnover situation, the organisation has to establish the level of turnover, the cost of this turnover and the reasons for it. We explore the different methods available for investigating the reason for turnover below, but for now let us turn our attention to determining levels and costs.

In terms of measuring the level of turnover in a company, a variety of quantitative methods are often used, the most common being the following:

- crude turnover rate calculation – establishing the percentage of the workforce to have left in a year
- stability rate calculation – establishing how long people tend to remain in the organisation. This is important because the action that should be taken if the company tends to lose most people in the first few months of employment is different from the action that should be taken if it is losing people with a considerable length of service
- cohort analysis – establishing the stability rate of one specific group/cohort of employees (such as a specific year's graduate intake) so that the retention of these staff over time can be tracked.

A useful activity to undertake after such calculations is benchmarking – which can be either internal or external. 'Internal benchmarking' refers to the practice of comparing the turnover levels in different areas of the business (to target turnover hotspots), or this year's level with that of previous years (to track trends over time, and monitor the success of retention initiatives). 'External benchmarking' refers to the practice of comparing the turnover level in the company either with national industry averages (via published survey data) or with the levels of turnover in companies in the same area (which can be accessed via forming 'benchmarking clubs' where such metrics are exchanged). Both types of benchmarking can help put turnover information into context. For example, if analysis revealed a turnover level of 10% in your organisation, this might be quite concerning – but it would be considerably less concerning if you knew that the average for your industry was 20%.

THE COSTS OF TURNOVER

Dysfunctional turnover can be extremely expensive for a business, the costs being both direct and indirect. It is important for HR practitioners to try to calculate the costs of dysfunctional turnover – both to understand the extent of the problem and also to gain commitment from senior management in relation to any proposed retention initiatives.

Survey data reveals that few organisations appear to make efforts to calculate what **labour turnover** actually costs them. The CIPD's 2010 Resourcing and Talent Planning survey reported that only 14% of the organisations surveyed were currently calculating the cost of labour turnover. One reason for this is the fact that calculating the costs of turnover is a very tricky business. Many of the elements, especially those relating to indirect costs, are not easily quantified; many organisations do not have the records needed; it is sometimes hard to distinguish between functional and dysfunctional turnover; and the activity can take a lot of time.

In many cases, a single instance of dysfunctional turnover may result in a vacancy being created which is filled externally. To arrive at an understanding of the overall cost of this, we must consider a variety of issues:

Table 3.1 Direct and indirect costs

Direct costs	Indirect costs
• HR administration time re the leaver • Costs of advertising the vacancy • HR administration time re the recruitment and selection process (sifting CVs, etc) • Selection expenses • Costs of covering the role while it is vacant (paying overtime to other staff or employing a temp) • HR administration time re the new starter • New starter costs • Induction and basic training costs	• Departing employee is less productive in final weeks • New employee is less productive in first few weeks • Loss of morale and productivity in colleagues if sad at departure or annoyed at increased workload • Possible damage to client relationships • Lack of return on investment in relation to any training and development that the departing employee was given • Company information could be used to the advantage of a competitor • Damage to company reputation (if individual leaves on bad terms or turnover level is high)

The simplest way to get an idea of the costs of dysfunctional turnover in general is to estimate the cost of turnover for a 'typical post' in the company, and then multiply this by the number of dysfunctional leavers for the year to reach a final 'dysfunctional turnover cost' for the year. Another approach is to estimate the total cost incurred by all activities related to employee resignation, recruitment, selection and induction over the course of a year – which includes both actual expenses and the cost of HR/management time.

UNDERSTANDING WHY PEOPLE LEAVE

In order to try to reduce levels of dysfunctional turnover, it is necessary to understand the reasons for it. People voluntarily decide to leave organisations for a wide range of reasons, and the first important distinction to be made is between turnover that is unavoidable and that which could have been avoided. Unavoidable turnover refers to circumstances such as ill health, domestic commitments, moving house or returning to study – where the decision to leave has nothing to do with the company and is therefore out of management's control. Avoidable turnover, however, applies to departures that are caused by some form of dissatisfaction – meaning that it is potentially within management's control. It has been estimated that around 90% of employee departures fall into this category.

If 90% of voluntary resignations could potentially be avoided by the use of appropriate organisational interventions, it is important to do a bit more digging into the factors that are causing these departures, so that the appropriate interventions can be identified. Rather than making assumptions about the causes of turnover (such as assuming that it is all about the rate of pay), a number of qualitative data sources can be used to identify the real reasons. The most common sources of information tend to be exit interviews and general staff satisfaction surveys.

According to a recent CIPD survey, around 90% of organisations make use of some sort of exit interview mechanism – a discussion between the departing employee and a company representative (usually the line manager or a member of the HR team) focused on reasons for leaving, factors that might have encouraged the individual to stay, and improvements that the organisation can make moving forward. Some companies use a questionnaire rather than a face-to-face discussion.

REFLECTIVE ACTIVITY

It is important to be aware that the information collected in an exit interview may not be 100% reliable, especially where the discussion takes place between an employee and their own line manager near to their date of departure.

1   What issues might influence the likelihood that an employee will be completely honest in their exit interview?

The annual employee attitude or staff satisfaction survey is another useful tool in understanding turnover. This is a mechanism designed for the frequent and systematic gathering of opinions on a broad range of organisation-wide issues from the entire workforce. Such surveys can help an organisation target retention initiatives appropriately because they highlight potential sources of satisfaction and dissatisfaction in all employees, rather than just those who have already decided to leave.

Other methods that can be used include surveys of ex-employees (completed a couple of months after departure), analysis of 'stayers' to see what factors encourage people to remain with the company, and 'last job move' surveys – asking new employees to talk about why they left their last job. Although the latter will not provide information on what your own company is doing right or wrong as an employer, it will provide information on the specific dynamics that operate in key labour markets.

RETENTION STRATEGIES

Once you have ascertained the level of turnover (especially dysfunctional turnover), how much it is costing and the main reasons, you are in a position to start to develop an appropriate retention strategy. There are three key issues here. The first is securing senior management support for the strategy; the second is identifying the appropriate initiatives; and the third is ensuring alignment. The latter refers to three different forms of alignment – alignment between individual retention initiatives; alignment between the retention strategy and other HR strategies; and alignment with overall organisation strategy.

Because most retention strategies require the investment of considerable financial and human resources – in terms of planning, development, execution and maintenance – it is important that the HR department makes a strong business case outlining the need for action. It is here that the costing calculations will prove most useful – showing exactly how much money employee turnover is costing the company, and how much could be saved were this level to be reduced. To make sure the issue is given the prominence it deserves, HR departments should aim to include turnover information (along with other key metrics) in monthly HR reports that can be discussed at senior management meetings or be added to the board report.

In terms of the specific initiatives to be included in the strategy, a wide range of things can be considered, the usefulness of each and the most effective combination being dependent entirely on the nature of the turnover issue in the organisation.

A breakdown of common reasons for leaving and their associated retention initiatives is presented in Table 3.2 below.

Table 3.2 Reasons for leaving, with associated retention initiatives

Reason for leaving	Retention initiatives
Lack of development opportunities	Regular employee appraisals Investment in training and development (various forms) Skills development programmes (linked to succession planning) Lateral as well as vertical moves
Bad relationships with supervisors or colleagues	Investment in management training Developing an internal mediation scheme Communication and team-building activities Opportunities for internal transfers

Reason for leaving	Retention initiatives
Negative opinion of the company in general	Transparency in policies and procedures Communication initiatives Consultation and involvement initiatives A focus on equal opportunities and diversity Investment in ethics and corporate social responsibility (CSR) initiatives
Dissatisfaction with reward	External benchmarking with other companies to ensure that salaries are competitive An internal job evaluation procedure to ensure that reward is equitably distributed A flexible benefits scheme from which each employee can select the package that best suits their needs A focus on intrinsic rewards – job variety, autonomy, etc
Incompatibility of work with other commitments	Flexible working arrangements (hours/location) Assistance for working mothers (investing in a crèche or childcare vouchers, etc) Sabbaticals
Dissatisfaction with the working environment	Investment in maintenance and equipment

In addition to this, because a lot of turnover occurs in the first six months of a new role, it is essential that effective induction and transition mechanisms are in place.

Finally, it is important that the retention strategy is fully communicated to all levels of the management structure – because management has a crucial role in the implementation and consistency of many of the component initiatives. It is also important to communicate any policy changes to all employees – to ensure that they are aware of all of the provisions, and so that they feel their opinions (perhaps as the result of satisfaction surveys) are being listened to and acted on.

THE ROLE OF THE PSYCHOLOGICAL CONTRACT

One concept that is relevant to understanding controllable dysfunctional turnover is the psychological contract. Whereas the employment contract sets out the explicit commitments between an employer and employee (pay for hours worked, etc), the psychological contract refers to the more implicit commitments. The CIPD factsheet on the subject (CIPD, 2012b) defines it as 'the perceptions of the two parties, employee and employer, of what their mutual obligations are towards each other'. These obligations are often informal and imprecise, but tend to be seen as 'promises' and 'expectations'.

The psychological contract is relevant to employee turnover because of the concept of breach. When one party (usually the employer) fails to honour its side of the psychological contract, the other (usually the employee) perceives the contact to have been breached – resulting in feelings of anger, injustice, resentment and distrust.

A range of things can be seen to breach the psychological contract, but one of the main problems is unrealistic expectations – often the result of misleading messages in the recruitment process that cause people to compete for and subsequently accept jobs for which they are in truth unsuited. Ways to avoid unrealistic expectations include:

- ensuring that job descriptions are accurate
- ensuring that during job interviews, both employer and employee expectations are discussed
- offering a realistic job preview (such as an hour shadowing an individual doing the same job role, or a half-day working in the role)
- allowing team member involvement in the recruitment or selection process. Examples include Northamptonshire Police, who asked current staff to feature in podcasts for the company website, talking about their role and what they enjoyed about working for the organisation; and Prêt A Manger, who include the views of future colleagues in the selection process (after the candidates have all had a job preview with the team)
- considering recruitment from among the company's temps, interns, part-timers and others who are already familiar with the employer
- considering the use of an employee referral scheme. The idea is that the current employee knows both the company and the candidate well, and will know where there is a good fit.

 Does reality match the rhetoric?

CASE STUDY

On the topic of employer branding above, we noted the claim made by Google that they offer employees freedom, collaboration and an environment that fosters 'health and happiness'. But is this in fact the reality of working there? The following article extract suggests it might not be – at least, not for all staff.

'In 2008 Google HR set up a private Google Group to ask former employees why they left the company ... The thread shows a brutal honesty about what it's like to work at Google, at least from the point of view of employees who were unhappy enough to resign. [There were a number of complaints ...] but one message stands out in most of the posts – employees thought they were entering the promised land when they joined Google, and most of them were disappointed. Some of them wondered if it meant they were somehow lacking ... "If you can't be happy there, how will you ever be happy? If you can't be productive there, how will you ever be productive?"' (Arrington, 2009)

As well as unfulfilled expectations, a range of things can result in a breach of the psychological contract, including a sudden shock or a gradual erosion of the contract as a result of repeated minor violations. In terms of the former, Table 3.3 indicates the sort of shock that might be experienced, and the breach it represents.

Table 3.3 Shocks resulting in perceived breaches of the psychological contract

Sudden shock issue	The breach
Company reorganisation and possible redundancies	Security
Being passed over for promotion	Career enhancement; equity
Abusive treatment by line manager	Trust and respect
Overtime freeze	Remuneration expectations
Relocation	Work–life balance
Changed working hours	Work–life balance
Manager takes credit for your work	Recognition and reward

MANAGING RETIREMENT, DISMISSAL AND REDUNDANCY

In the last section we looked at employee turnover - primarily considering the issue of **voluntary turnover**. Before we complete this chapter, it is important for you to be aware of three other types of employee departure: retirement, dismissal and redundancy.

RETIREMENT

'Retirement' traditionally referred to the scheduled departure of an employee from the company because he or she had reached the set age for departure from the overall workforce – which was either 60 (women) or 65 (men) years old. Due to developments in employment law, however, individual employees have a lot more control in the retirement process today. It is no longer lawful for companies to compulsorily retire employees at a certain age unless there is a genuine reason (a justified way of achieving a legitimate business aim), and many individuals choose to take flexible retirement options when the time feels right, rather than leaving the workforce altogether.

If an individual becomes unable to meet the needs of the job role through factors related to age, any exit should therefore be managed through the performance and capability procedure.

Good practice in the management of retirement is for there to be ongoing discussions with all employees about their future intentions, and the offer of a range of options when retirement starts to be considered. The range may include the following:

- moving from a full-time to a part-time contract
- stepping down to a role with slightly less responsibility
- winding down – gradually reducing working hours
- atypical contracts, perhaps including an extended period of leave
- retiring from permanent employment but remaining on the company books as a consultant.

Such options have proved very popular. In a survey carried out by the Centre for Research into Older Workers (CROW), it was found that 80% of the respondents (people currently in full-time work) would like to stay in work beyond their expected retirement dates. Only 9% would like to do so on a full-time basis, while most would like to stay on only if they could work part-time, occasionally or on a consultancy basis (CIPD, 2011: 12).

DISMISSAL

Along with redundancy (covered below), 'dismissal' refers to **involuntary employee turnover** – where the employment contract is terminated by the employer. Dismissals refer to situations in which employment is terminated because the employee has failed to meet the requirements of the job role. The key issues when managing dismissals are that there is a valid reason for the dismissal, and that a fair and proper procedure is followed.

A valid reason for dismissal tends to fall into one of two categories: conduct or capability. Conduct issues relate to the breaking of company rules in either a minor way (misconduct) or a major way (gross misconduct). Capability issues refer to an inability to do the job – which might be due to either competence or health.

In terms of procedure, the standards expected for dismissals are laid out in the Acas Codes of Practice. More details on this, together with information on the legal claims that can be made by individuals should they feel they have been dismissed unfairly, are set out in Chapter 2, *Employment Law*.

REDUNDANCY

The second type of involuntary turnover is redundancy. This refers to a dismissal because the job role that the individual performs is no longer viable. The definition of 'redundancy' is set out in Section 139(1) of the Employment Rights Act 1996, but in summary, a redundancy only occurs where there has been, or is going to be, a closure of the business, a closure of the workplace or a diminution in the need for employees doing work of a certain kind.

It is good practice for employees to try to find alternatives to compulsory redundancy. This is obviously preferable for the workforce, but it can also have benefits for the company (in terms of staff morale, reputation and ability to expand in the future). Alternatives to redundancy include the following, some of which may be offered by a company as a matter of course, whereas others may instead be introduced via consultation with the workforce:

- recruitment freeze and redeployment of existing talent (with re-training) where vacancies arise
- overtime freeze
- pay cuts
- reduced days/hours
- sabbaticals
- voluntary redundancy
- voluntary early retirement.

Voluntary options at KPMG

In December 2008, amid concerns over the financial climate and while key competitors were announcing plans to cut hundreds of jobs, Big Four accounting firm KPMG launched an innovative scheme to cut down on wage costs without resorting to redundancy. The firm gave its UK staff the option of applying to work a four- day week (with the fifth unpaid) or take a sabbatical of up to 12 weeks (at 30% pay) – something that proved highly popular, with more than 85% of employees signing up for the scheme until the end of 2010.

When such alternatives have been exhausted, and redundancy is the only option, it is important that a company follows the correct procedure for redundancies. More information is available on the legal requirements of this in the *Employment Law* chapter (Chapter 2) of this book. It is important for a company to be as communicative and transparent as possible in such circumstances, and to pay attention to those who remain employed (in terms of reassurance and the monitoring of workloads, etc) as well as those who are dismissed.

  Happy Dog wants happy staff

Happy Dog is a small chain of hot-dog cafés in Sundale Valley, a rural area that covers three villages and lots of open countryside. The population of Sundale Valley is largely retirees and families (because it has good schools and good transport links with the local city for employment), and is a popular family-day-out destination because of the number of beautiful walking routes in the area.

Happy Dog has enjoyed a steady staff turnover for the three years since it opened, and has successfully operated as an Employer of Churn – being especially popular with the large number of sixth-form students in the area, and university students looking for work during summer holidays (when demand for workers at Happy Dog tends to increase owing to tourism).

A new out-of-town retail and entertainment complex is being built in the area, however, which will include a cinema, a ten-pin bowling alley, a number of fashion stores and two fast-food outlets that are both part of well-established national chains. Mr Terrier, the manager of Happy Dog, is quite concerned because he has seen adverts in the local Job Centre advertising the following roles in these outlets: kitchen assistants, serving staff and cleaning staff. Mr Terrier is worried because these match the roles in his outlets, the rate of pay is the same, and the benefits will be especially appealing to the local student population: discounts at all entertainment and retail outlets in the complex, and a guaranteed location flexibility policy (so that students can transfer to a different outlet in the chain during university term-time).

Because Happy Dog does not have its own HR function, Mr Terrier has called you up for some advice. He wants to know how he can ensure that his outlets have suitable staff without having to increase pay rates – something he simply cannot afford to do.

Questions

1   In addition to sixth-form students, who else would you advise Mr Terrier to target as potential employees?

2   What provisions could he introduce to make employment at Happy Dog more attractive to both students and other groups, without being too costly?

3   How could he gauge the success of new provisions?

FURTHER READING

CIPD (2012) Information Pages [Online]. Information pages are available on the website, which provide factsheets, podcasts and survey reports on each of the following topics:

- Labour market: http://www.cipd.co.uk/hr-topics/labour-market.aspx
- Recruitment: http://www.cipd.co.uk/hr-topics/recruitment.aspx
- Employer branding: http://www.cipd.co.uk/hr-topics/employer-branding.aspx
- Selection and assessment: http://www.cipd.co.uk/hr-topics/selection-assessment.aspx
- Retention and turnover: http://www.cipd.co.uk/hr-topics/retention-turnover.aspx
- Redundancy: http://www.cipd.co.uk/hr-topics/redundancy.aspx
- Dismissal: http://www.cipd.co.uk/hr-topics/dismissal.aspx

Various publications on the topic of the UK labour market are available from the Office for National Statistics: http://www.statistics.gov.uk/hub/labour-market/index.html

Related to the topic of dismissals, a key resource for HR professionals is the Acas Code of Practice on the recommended procedures for conducting disciplinary and grievance investigations. The relevant document – Code of Practice 1 (April 2009) – can be accessed at: http://www.acas.org.uk/media/ pdf/h/m/ Acas_Code_of_Practice_1_on_disciplinary_and_grievance_procedures.pdf

The following CIPD textbooks also provide more detail on the subjects covered in this chapter:

Taylor, S. (2011) *Resourcing and Talent Planning*. London, CIPD. Contains detailed chapters on most of the issues covered above.

Taylor, S. (2012) *Contemporary Issues in HRM*. London, CIPD. Especially useful for information related to the labour market and other pertinent trends in the external environment.

REFERENCES

Arrington, M. (2009) 'Why Google employees quit'. Available at: http://tech crunch.com/2009/01/18/why-google-employees-quit/ [accessed Feb. 2012].

Atkinson, J. (1984a) *Flexibility, Uncertainty and Manpower Management*, IMS Report No.89. Brighton, Institute of Manpower Studies.

Atkinson, J. (1984b) 'Manpower strategies for flexible organisations', *Personnel Management*, August: 28–31.

BIS (2010) 'Skills for sustainable growth', Strategy document, Department for Business, Innovation and Skills. Available at: http://www.bis.gov.uk/assets/ biscore/ further-education-skills/docs/s/10-1274-skills-for-sustainable-growth-strategy.pdf [accessed March 2012].

CIPD (2009) *Recruitment, Retention and Turnover*, Annual Survey Report. London, Chartered Institute of Personnel and Development.

CIPD (2011) *Managing Age*, Guide. London, Chartered Institute of Personnel and Development.

CIPD (2012a) 'Succession planning', Factsheet. London, Chartered Institute of Personnel and Development.

CIPD (2012b) 'The psychological contract', Factsheet. London, Chartered Institute of Personnel and Development.

Higgs, M (2004) 'Future Trends in HRM' in: Rees, D and McBain, R (eds) *People Management: Challenges and Opportunities*. Basingstoke, Palgrave Macmillan.

Industrial Relations Services (IRS) (2003) 'Setting the tone: job descriptions and person specifications', *Employment Review* No. 776: 42–8.

Leitch, Lord S. (2006) 'Leitch Review of Skills: Final Report'. Available at: http:// www. delni.gov.uk/leitch_finalreport051206[1]-2.pdf [accessed March 2012].

Lievens, F., Van Hoye, G. and Anseel, F. (2007) 'Organizational identity and employer image: towards a unifying framework', *British Journal of Management*, 18: 45–59.

People Management [Online] (2009) 'KPMG employees get flexible', Latest HR News, 26 March.

CHAPTER 4

Employee Engagement

Ted Johns

CHAPTER CONTENTS

KEY LEARNING OUTCOMES

By the end of this chapter, you should be able to:

- understand the concept of employee engagement and its importance as a contributor to positive corporate and performance outcomes

- analyse what is distinctive about employee engagement when contrasted with other related concepts, such as employee involvement

- identify and critically assess the findings of recent studies that purport to demonstrate the incidence of employee engagement in various organisations, industries and sectors, both public and private

- evaluate the processes through which high levels of employee engagement can be secured and sustained within organisations

- implement HR strategies and practices intended to raise levels of employee engagement in a specific organisational context

- explain the principles and applications of high-performance working (HPW) and the role of employee engagement as an element in the realisation of an HPW culture

- outline the future for employee engagement, principally throughout the UK economy but also within the globalised world of work.

INTRODUCTION AND OVERVIEW

Many years ago the philosopher Sir Isaiah Berlin wrote an essay, 'The hedgehog and the fox', in which he identified two types of thinkers. The fox, cunning and resourceful, knows many things; the hedgehog, diligent and persevering, knows one big thing.

Organisations are the same. They often focus on one big thing – namely, profitability. The public sector is more nebulous because it can't focus on profitability, but it can concentrate on resource efficiencies, service delivery and customer feedback. Organisations begin by claiming to know how to make the company grow, and then work from the top down to get the job done, by building factories, organising offices, creating websites and selling their products. This can work, provided the vision is brilliant and the execution flawless. But it often falls apart further down the chain of command, especially when front-line managers and customer-facing employees don't share the high-level vision (why should they?) and start picking holes in it, deliberately or otherwise.

The problem is that the hedgehog's insular vision tends to ignore the importance of people as contributors to business success, whereas the fox celebrates them. It's the quality of those millions of one-to-one interactions between manager and employee, and between employee and customer, that typically distinguish the businesses that thrive from those that founder. These are what Jan Carlzon, CEO of SAS, the Scandinavian Airlines System, described as the 'moments of truth' – occurring perhaps 50,000 times a day when staff interact with each other and/or with customers, at events. This is why for employees whose contents cannot be regulated, controlled or micro-managed by their organisations, engagement is important. When employees are engaged their managers can be confident that they will conduct themselves in the interests of the business. There can be no such confidence about the behaviour of employees who are not engaged or who, even worse, are actively disengaged.

Employee engagement is one of those HR topics that could endure to the point where chapters about engagement become a compulsory feature in all respectable HRM textbooks – or it could disappear off the face of the earth in a little while, after all its manifold facets have been exhausted. What you have to do is go through this chapter and determine your answers to these questions:

- Is employee engagement something genuinely new, or is it simply a reworking or a rehash of old ideas dressed up (typically by consultants) to look as if it is something new?
- Is the notion of employee engagement sufficiently different from similar notions such as 'involvement', 'participation' and 'commitment'?
- Is there any worthwhile evidence to show that organisations that consciously strive to produce a workforce that is 'engaged' will then experience superior performance and profitability outcomes – or are the arguments about the supposed benefits of employee engagement simply founded on plausible logic and 'common sense', but nothing more?

We can answer the first of the questions straight away, because it is now widely accepted by both practitioners and academics that employee engagement is not merely a fad (Schaufeli and Bakker, 2010). This is because there is an enormous momentum of accumulating evidence that high levels of employee engagement have a significant and positive impact at both organisational and individual levels.

WHAT IS EMPLOYEE ENGAGEMENT?

The first thing we must do is define what we're talking and writing about. And that's where our problems begin, because there are several definitions we could use, and none of them is absolutely definitive.

In its Factsheet on *Employee Engagement*, the CIPD (2009) describes employee engagement as 'a combination of commitment to the organisation and its values plus a willingness to help out colleagues (organisational citizenship)'. So far, so good – and the CIPD definition continues:

> It goes beyond job satisfaction and is not simply motivation. Engagement is something the employee has to offer: it cannot be 'required' as part of the employment contract.

MacLeod and Clarke (2009) build on the ideas of David Guest in constructing their own model of employee engagement

> as a workplace approach designed to ensure that employees are committed to their organisation's goals and values, motivated to contribute to organisational success and able to enhance their own sense of well-being.

Interviewed for a *People Management* article, MacLeod (2009) also argues that employee engagement goes to 'the heart of the workplace relationship between employer and employee' and that it can be

> a key to unlocking productivity and transforming the working lives of many people for whom Monday morning is an especially low part of the week.

Kahn (1990), writing when the concept of employee engagement was but a gleam in some inventive and ambitious academic's armoury, defined 'personal engagement' as the 'harnessing of organisation members' selves to their work roles'. By contrast, and writing more specifically about engagement at work, Schaufeli and Salanova (2007) define the concept as 'a positive, fulfilling, work-related state of mind that is characterised by vigour, dedication and absorption'. Each of these components is further explained as follows:

- vigour: high levels of energy and mental resilience while working, the willingness to invest effort in one's work, and persistence even in the face of difficulties
- dedication: strong involvement in one's work, and experiencing a sense of significance, enthusiasm, inspiration, pride and challenge
- absorption: being fully concentrated and happily engrossed in one's work, whereby time passes quickly and one has difficulty detaching oneself from work.

For the purposes of a recent study entitled 'Management competencies for enhancing employee engagement', the CIPD (2011) define employee engagement in perhaps the best way possible:

> Being focused in what you do (thinking), feeling good about yourself in your role and the organisation (feeling), and acting in a way that demonstrates commitment to the organisational values and objectives (acting).

WHAT IS DISTINCTIVE ABOUT EMPLOYEE ENGAGEMENT?

One of the concepts closely related to employee engagement is organisational commitment, which loosely refers to an individual's psychological attachment to the organisation. Commitment can be contrasted with other work-related attitudes, such as 'job satisfaction' (the employee's feelings about his or her work) and 'organisational identification' (the degree to which the employee feels a sense of 'oneness' with the organisation, and therefore doesn't see any appreciable difference between his or her own self-interests and the interests of the employer).

There are three 'mindsets' that can characterise an individual's commitment to his or her organisation

- *affective commitment* – This refers to the employee's positive emotional attachment to the organisation. An employee who is affectively committed strongly identifies with the goals of the business and wishes to remain a part of it (and them). Such employees commit to the organisation because they 'want to', so in that sense this psychological condition is very similar to the CIPD's own definition of employee engagement – i.e. it is something that employees have to 'offer', and it cannot therefore be part of the employment contract.
- *continuance commitment* – This kind of commitment is more negative in character, because these individuals commit to the organisation on account of the perceived 'costs' of departure and loss. These 'costs' include straightforward economic costs (such as pension rights) but also embrace social costs (friendship links with work colleagues) and personal costs (fear of insecurity

and unemployment). Such committed employees remain members of the organisation because they 'have to'.

- *normative commitment* – These individuals commit to and remain with the organisation because of feelings of obligation and indebtedness. For example, if the employer has invested resources in training and developing the employee, the employee then feels a 'moral' obligation to put forth effort and stay in the organisation at least until the 'debt' is repaid. These employees remain committed to the organisation because they feel they 'ought to'.

It has been shown that engaged workers are characterised by low levels of 'burnout', as well as by low levels of neuroticism and high levels of extraversion when compared with the overall features of a typical workforce. Some researchers go further by suggesting that workers with high levels of engagement also enjoy good mental and physical health, again in comparison with their colleagues.

Engagement may be about behaviour, but ultimately and even more importantly it is about performance, results and outcomes. Harnessing the discretionary effort of people produces better results than if people simply work within the confines of their job descriptions. When individuals 'go the extra mile', it makes sense to believe that teams, divisions, departments and organisations will work more effectively, customers will receive better service, and efficiency will improve.

As always, however, we must keep our feet on the ground. Employee engagement does not follow automatically from feelings of job satisfaction and happiness. A person can be happy at work and satisfied with the job because the tasks being performed are intrinsically challenging – but it may still be the case that no meaningful work is being performed. So job satisfaction and happiness do not in themselves create high performance.

WHAT ARE THE COMPONENTS OF EMPLOYEE ENGAGEMENT, AND HOW IS IT LINKED WITH HR POLICIES, STRATEGIES AND PRACTICES?

Looked at in the round, there are at root two basic, competing views about the ways of achieving high levels of employee engagement.

The first is the bottom-up philosophy and takes the line that levels of engagement are primarily a function of employees' experiences at work. Do they enjoy what they do? Do they receive adequate training? Is their performance evaluated fairly? Are they involved in the key decisions that affect them? From this perspective we can see that engagement is largely the result of factors controlled partly by the technology (in the case of production flows) but principally by team leaders, supervisors and junior management.

The second view is the top-down philosophy, which contends that engagement is reinforced chiefly by the behaviour and role-modelling (deliberate or not) of the organisation's top-level leaders. The best-managed and best-led organisations are typically characterised by a unifying vision, which encapsulates what the business is trying to achieve, a rationale for the changes being pursued and a picture of what the future organisation will look like. Part of this vision, too, is likely to comprise a statement of the core values for the organisation and what is expected of employees.

All these components together comprise a 'Big Idea', which Purcell and his colleagues (2003) describe as

> a simple way of expressing some basic assumptions about what the organisation is and how it works … If it is embedded, enduring and connects the inside with the outside, it is very likely to be habitual – that is, seen as normal shared practice.

The Big Idea concept reflects a strong, inclusive culture inside the organisation plus strong, positive relationships with customers, employees and other stakeholders. Examples include 'mutuality', the Big Idea for the Nationwide Building Society (Purcell *et al*, 2003), and what Vineet Nayar (2010) describes as 'EFCS' (Employees First, Customers Second), the Big Idea of IT company HCL Technologies.

So the questions we need to ask, when reviewing a top-down philosophy for employee engagement, are these: Does the top management communicate a compelling Big Idea? Do they supply a clear sense of direction? Do they set firm priorities? Do they consistently and continuously promote the values, principles and actions associated with engagement? Do they, above all, operate with integrity?

Undoubtedly, the creation of a high-engagement culture depends on both a bottom-up and a top-down alliance. However, research reported by Roger Maitland (2004) suggests that the engagement levels of top performers in any organisation are primarily driven by the behaviours of high-level leaders rather than by the activities of first-line managers and supervisors. This contrasts with the situation for poor and average performers, where a worker's engagement levels are slightly more likely to be influenced by his or her immediate managers. So the moral here is that you must have everyone pulling together, but the more senior people must pull that little bit harder than anyone else.

Certainly, recent research emphasises the role of managers in promoting an engagement culture. Robinson and Hayday (2009), on behalf of the Institute of Employment Studies (IES), have reported on a project designed to understand how managers who inspire and engage their teams to perform behave. From seven participating organisations the IES identified 25 'engaging managers' who had little in common except their ability to engage their teams through very similar behaviours. Their jobs and roles varied, their spans of control ranged from four people to over 5,000, and they were very different in terms of personality, background and training. But what was spectacular was that their behaviours were broadly the same:

- They communicate and make clear what is expected ('I try to encourage people to think of the wider objectives … and how they fit in').
- They listen, value and involve their teams.
- They focus on targets rather than on processes, tasks and procedures.
- They have, and share, a clear strategic vision.

- They show an active interest in others.
- They exercise good leadership skills, especially through positive role-modelling.
- They act with respect, and in turn are respected.

The managers in the sample were put forward by their organisations because their teams had high engagement scores. Yet it soon became apparent that these were also high-performing managers with high-performing teams. It was also noticeable that these managers were good at the difficult stuff, like tackling poor performance quickly and effectively, and breaking bad news.

As well as describing engagement behaviours, respondents to the IES study were also asked to describe the behaviours of managers who were disengaging:

- They lack empathy and any interest in people.
- They fail to listen and communicate.
- They are self-centred.
- They don't motivate or inspire.
- They blame others when mistakes are made, and don't take responsibility for team actions and results.
- They are typically aggressive.
- They lack personal awareness (of how their behaviour impacts on others).
- They don't deliver on promises.

 REFLECTIVE ACTIVITY

In the IES research discussed here, team members were asked to draw pictures that represented how they saw their managers.

Several themes emerged. The most popular picture of all, however, was of a sun or a smiling face.

Try drawing a picture which symbolises how you see a manager you have either worked for *or have observed in action.* If you are in touch with colleagues who also know the manager you have chosen to draw, ask them to do the same (without showing them your picture first).

1   Analyse the results. To what extent do the pictures reinforce each other?

2   Could you see yourself showing these pictures to the manager? If not, why not?

Members of the engaged teams enjoyed their work and looked forward to coming to work. Above all, they felt they shared an open culture and an ability to discuss a wide range of topics, with comments like, 'You can almost see a visual difference between the teams.'

According to Patterson and his colleagues (1997), there are 13 processes that we would expect to find in any organisation that is characterised by a 'high engagement' culture. Note that these 13 processes are also thought to be relevant for **high-performance working** (HPW), a topic pursued later in this chapter.

- 'appropriate' recruitment and selection systems, going beyond mere legal compliance

- comprehensive induction programmes, socialising new entrants into the organisation's core values (which in any case should feature in all recruitment literature, advertising, online briefings and application forms)
- sophisticated and wide provision for 'learning' (previously known as 'training')
- coherent, co-ordinated and 'bundled' performance management with customer-driven progress measures – 'bundled' in the sense that the entire performance management system operates to the same criteria. Note here, too, that the term 'performance management' refers to all the systems and processes through which the behaviour of employees is incentivised towards the accomplishment of corporate purposes; it does not simply describe ways of dealing with poor performers
- skills development within the workforce that is based on flexibility, multi-skilling and 'employability' – i.e. equipping employees with the knowledge and skills they will need to fill any vacancies required in the future
- jobs characterised where possible by intrinsic variety and individual responsibility for outcomes, with expectations about 'discretionary behaviour'. This in turn means a preference for accountability profiles (which define job outputs) rather than conventional job descriptions (which focus on task performance)
- teamwork, collaboration within and between corporate departments and functions, with no evidence of a 'silo' mentality
- frequent and comprehensive communications to, from and with employees, in order to maximise involvement and 'employee voice', generating a sense of ownership for performance and corporate results
- quality-improvement programmes with cross-functional co-operation to ensure that strategic alignment and 'bundling' are not damaged or undermined
- harmonised terms and conditions throughout the enterprise
- market-competitive levels of pay and overall remuneration (including benefits) plus interpersonal recognition by managers who practise 'management by appreciation'
- rewards related to individual and group progress, success and achievement, measured in relation to the organisation's high-level purposes, vision and Big Idea
- policies and practices intended to enhance work–life balance.

The main driver of engagement, say Robinson and Hayday (2009), is a sense of feeling valued and involved. The main components of this are:

- involvement in decision-making – especially about issues of immediate relevance to the workforce
- freedom to voice ideas ('employee voice') to managers who take the trouble and time to listen to them
- feeling enabled to perform well
- having opportunities to develop the job – and in the job
- feeling that the organisation is concerned for employees' health and well-being.

WHAT ARE THE BENEFITS FOR ORGANISATIONS, THEIR PEOPLE AND THEIR CUSTOMERS?

All sorts of sometimes extravagant claims are made about the organisational results achieved by organisations characterised by high levels of employee engagement throughout their workforces.

For example, Sarah Lewis (2011) assertively promises that 'Engaged workers perform better and give extra discretionary effort,' while the CIPD Factsheet on *Employee Engagement* (2009) says that 'Employers want engaged employees because they deliver improved business performance.'

CASE STUDY

 Try something new today

Gwyn Burr, previously customer service director at supermarket Sainsbury's, has been put in charge of the HR function as well. She points out that 'Colleagues and customers are inextricably linked ... Every touch point that we have between a customer and a colleague is a people interaction. Therefore I'm a big believer in engaging our colleagues. Having engaged colleagues leads to excellence in customer service.'

This philosophy has led Burr to try something new, by using the principle behind the company's tried and tested customer engagement technique ('universal customer appeal') and

applying it to staff ('universal colleague appeal'). The aim is to put the customer and the staff at the heart of everything that Sainsbury's does.

Burr has slightly re-aligned the reporting relationships in the Sainsbury's HR department so that her team now has three HR directors rather than the previous five: these directors are responsible for retail HR, central HR, and colleague engagement, so engagement has a director all to itself. That's how important it is in this company.

Source: Churchard (2011)

One of the most significant research reports supporting the positive impact of employee engagement is the Towers Watson 2007/2008 Global Workforce study (2009), which clearly demonstrates the links between high engagement and high performance. Observing 50 global organisations over a one-year period, this investigation found that organisations with high employee engagement levels benefited from a 19% increase in operating income, whereas organisations with low levels of engagement saw a 32% drop. The same report also found that organisations with highly engaged workforces experienced a 28% growth in earnings per share, compared with an 11% decline in earnings per share for organisations with low levels of engagement.

Other research has shown that high levels of employee engagement are positively associated with organisational commitment (Saks, 2006), customer satisfaction, employee loyalty, profitability, productivity and even safety (Harter *et al*, 2002). Those employees who feel themselves to be engaged typically experience greater job satisfaction (irrespective of the specific nature of the jobs they perform) and greater well-being (Schaufeli *et al*, 2008; Alfes *et al*, 2010). It is also claimed that engaged employees are more likely to act as organisational advocates than non-engaged or disengaged employees, and can therefore play a powerful role in promoting their organisation as an employer of choice (employer brand).

In reality, however plausible such claims – about the causal relationships between employee engagement and corporate profits and profitability – may be, in many cases they cannot be verified because crucial information is not made public by the consultancy firms from which many such claims originate. An exception is the Gallup Organization, which has shown in a study based on nearly 8,000 business units of 36 companies that those units in the top 25% on 'work engagement' produced 1% to 4% higher profitability and had, on average, between $80,000 and $120,000 higher monthly revenues or sales than the units in the bottom 25%. This translates into a difference of at least $960,000 per year per business unit.

Indeed, several Gallup studies have demonstrated the massive benefits to be gained when employee engagement and customer engagement are pursued in tandem, especially given the belief that each can feed off the other (either positively or negatively). For an American clothing retailer, Gallup has been able to show that stores that strove to satisfy both customers and employees had significantly better profit margins than stores that focused on just one objective or the other. It is worth noting that similar results have been reported by Hutchinson and Purcell (2003) when comparing four matched Tesco stores in the UK. As in most retailers, performance is measured by something called the conversion rate, which is the percentage of customers who actually buy something. Stores that scored in the top of the Gallup measures in terms of both customer satisfaction and employee engagement had much higher conversion rates than stores scoring at the bottom.

Faced with the undeniable significance of these results, the manager of one low-scoring store in the study made some changes. Ordinarily, a manager might ask a retail employee to check stock, clean up dressing rooms or work at the cash desk. This top-down system does little to encourage employee engagement and does nothing to enhance the customer's experience – so the manager decided to give staff the freedom to respond to customer needs on their own. When they noticed that the changing rooms were filling up, for example, some employees moved to the cash registers, anticipating that customers who were trying on clothes were about to make purchases. This pleased customers, because they didn't have to wait a long time to pay, and it made employees happy because they were felt they were making a difference (Fleming and Harter, 2001).

Other studies, principally involving specialised groups of respondents, have suggested similar positive outcomes linked to employee engagement. Some examples are listed below:

● Where staff in hotels and restaurants are engaged, their actions lead to better service quality as measured by customers – the people who ultimately matter most (Salanova *et al*, 2005a).

- In the USA, evidence among university students shows that the more engaged students produce higher Grade Point Average scores (Salanova *et al*, 2005b).
- The higher the level of engagement among cabin service staff in airlines, the better is their in- and extra-role performance on each flight (Xanthopoulou *et al*, 2008).
- In the US beverage company MolsonCoors, it was found that engaged employees were five times less likely than non-engaged employees to have a safety incident and seven times less likely to have a lost-time safety incident. In fact, the average cost of a safety incident for an engaged employee was $63, compared with an average of $392 for non-engaged employees (Lockwood, 2007).

Such evidence appears pretty conclusive. However, we must be cautious and even sceptical before we automatically accept that employee engagement yields superior corporate outcomes. First of all, profits and profitability depend on many complex and complicated considerations, some inside the business and some outside, and to rely on monocausal explanations for a single outcome is notoriously dangerous and potentially very misleading. Second, there may be other factors which produce both high levels of employee engagement and superior levels of profit and profitability, but which give the impression that there is a straightforward relationship between engagement and profit. Thus a small family business (like an Indian restaurant) may employ people who are very 'engaged' with the business – they are, after all, family members – and the business may be highly profitable – especially if the family members, being family members, aren't paid very much. But is employee engagement the cause, the only cause, the only single cause, of the restaurant's profitability?

Another problem concerns assumptions about the direction of causality. It seems to be taken for granted that employee engagement causes profitability to rise, but why shouldn't it be the other way round? After all, people like to be on the winning side, and if their company is doing well, it would make a lot of sense if they became more 'engaged' than if they found themselves unwilling conspirators on a sinking ship.

WHAT DOES THE RESEARCH TELL US ABOUT THE INCIDENCE OF EMPLOYEE ENGAGEMENT IN THE REAL WORLD?

In 2009, the CIPD commissioned Kingston University and Ipsos/MORI to undertake a national survey of employee attitudes, in an effort to discover the actual extent of engagement within the UK workforce (see CIPD, 2010). The results of this survey constitute a national benchmark against which employers can measure the findings of their own employee attitude surveys. However, it is worth injecting a note of caution here. Merely matching or exceeding the figures in a benchmark survey does not in itself justify any complacency, especially if you want to be a 'world-class' leading-edge business and therefore need to be ahead of the field rather than simply bunched in there with it. Also, you have to bear in mind the possibility that the benchmark may itself be low: as the CIPD (2009) itself concedes in its *Employee Engagement* Factsheet:

> Research confirms … that there is a significant gap between levels of engagement found among UK employees and those that would produce optimum performance.

Having issued these essential caveats, let's look at the results of the CIPD study. Overall, the report found that over a third of employees were actively engaged with their work – a rather higher figure than some other investigations have suggested. On looking in more detail at the three dimensions of engagement:

- *emotional engagement*, being very involved emotionally with one's work – This applied to around 60% of those in the CIPD sample
- *cognitive engagement*, focusing very hard while at work – A similar 60% said they were cognitively engaged
- *physical engagement*, being willing to go 'the extra mile' for the employer, and act discretionally to advance the employer's strategic goals – Here the figure was somewhat lower, at around 40%.

Other key results from the same research can be briefly outlined thus:

- More women than men were engaged with their work.
- Around a quarter of the under-35 group felt engaged, compared with about 40% among the over-35s.
- Almost half of managers were engaged, compared with around 30% of non-managers.
- Those on flexible contracts tended to be more emotionally engaged, more satisfied with their work, more likely to speak positively about their organisation and less likely to quit than those not employed on flexible contracts.
- Public sector employees were more likely to feel that their senior managers did not have a clear vision (a Big Idea) for the organisation, and, perhaps partly as a result, they had less trust and confidence in their senior managers. They were also less likely to believe the contents of organisational communications.

As with all survey results, especially those with a self-report and self-assessment content, the figures are capable of being interpreted in ways that do not necessarily support the most positive spin placed on them by the CIPD. For example, it is possible – perhaps even likely – that when employees are asked about the extent of their engagement with their work, they will be motivated to produce positive responses because if they don't, they are exposing themselves to the possibility of cognitive dissonance (i.e. doing one thing while saying something different).

Thus if people are asked how they feel about their work and express negative sentiments, they may begin to question their own actions: why stay in a job that you actively dislike? Of course, there are reasons for doing so – often depending on the poverty of the local labour market – but these reasons, brought into the conscious mind, can still make us feel uncomfortable. Much better, it seems, to reduce or eliminate the likelihood of cognitive dissonance by almost literally 'making the best of a bad job' and trying to find psychological and other benefits from a task that was initially entered purely for instrumental reasons.

Clearly, we cannot know for certain whether any of the CIPD respondents actually thought along these lines. It is highly likely that even if they had been asked, they might have denied it or refused to admit it, anyway. What is important is that when evaluating the extent of engagement among employees we must look further than employees' own self-assessments.

A significantly more negative picture of employee engagement in the UK economy emerged from a report by Marcus Buckingham (2001) involving a national sample of the UK working population. The research used the Gallup Q12 Index and produced the following results.

The most important primary finding from the Gallup research was that more than 80% of employees in the UK are not engaged at work. From the data, Gallup identified three distinct categories of employees:

- *engaged employees* – These are loyal, productive, less likely to leave, more inclined to recommend their employer as a place of work (and as a source of products or services, if appropriate) to friends and family
- *non-engaged employees* – These people may be productive, but they are not psychologically bonded to their organisation; they are more likely to defect to other employers
- *disengaged employees* – Such employees are physically present (assuming in fact that they have actually turned up for work in the first place) but psychologically absent; the only thing that enthuses them is the need to share with colleagues all the reasons why the organisation is such a rotten place to work.

Based on this classification, and bearing in mind once again that these results were achieved in 2001 using a particular methodology (although the Gallup Q12 instrument is a very strong device), Gallup found that only 17% of British workers were engaged, 63% were non-engaged and 20% were actively disengaged.

Not surprisingly, engaged employees looked on their employers much more positively than their actively disengaged colleagues did. Woody Allen once said that 80% of success is about showing up, so Gallup investigated attendance and absence figures. At the time, the engaged people in the sample missed, on average, 4.67 days of work a year, whereas actively disengaged employees missed 10.68 days. Gallup was also able to show that turnover levels among the engaged work groups were much lower than those of the actively disengaged groups.

The second most important finding was something that was definitely counter-intuitive. It was this: the longer employees stay with you, the less engaged they become. There is no easy explanation for this state of affairs, and it definitely contradicts one of the basic precepts of the human capital advantage model – namely, that human capital is one of the few assets that genuinely appreciates over time. Perhaps people really do become more valuable to the organisation – in terms of their skills, implicit knowledge, experience and so forth – but it is apparent from the Gallup results that these same people don't *feel* themselves to be more valuable.

As time goes on, and their work experience accumulates, they may encounter fewer opportunities for learning and challenge: so their lives become more predictable, more routinised, and therefore less adventurous and exciting. In such circumstances it would not be surprising if their engagement levels fell away.

HOW CAN WE DEVISE AND IMPLEMENT HR STRATEGIES AND PRACTICES THAT WILL RAISE LEVELS OF EMPLOYEE ENGAGEMENT?

The first essential point to acknowledge is that there has to be a compelling and convincing business case before any organisation should contemplate specific moves to create a genuinely engaged workforce. Merely doing it because it is thought to be 'good' for everyone involved will not work, for the following reasons:

- Not everyone in the organisation will support a principle of positive action for change being initiated merely because it sounds like a 'good' idea and will make everyone feel warm and comfortable inside. Some of those who won't support any such idea will hold very senior positions in the hierarchy and will therefore be in a position to block any engagement initiative that they think (rightly or wrongly) is being promoted for unjustified reasons.
- When organisations consider financial investments, they know that if any investment is to succeed, it must have a clear and unambiguous objective. Certainly the same is true of any organisational 'investment' in people, because if it is undertaken merely because it appears plausible, it sounds like a 'good' idea, or because it makes the organisation feel righteous, then it definitely won't work. So the presence of a business case for employee engagement is critical – and the strength of that business case must ultimately rest on the strong probability that higher levels of employee engagement will produce an investment return in terms of higher productivity, lower turnover, improved customer retention, and so forth. In turn, such evidence has to be persuasive and convincing, not merely founded on wishful thinking or people-focused rhetoric.

A strong business case can be constructed around any one or more of the following outcomes – and research evidence can always be found to bolster them:

- improved profitability and bottom-line results
- improved levels of customer satisfaction, customer loyalty, customer retention and new customer acquisition through the activities of 'advocate' customers
- reduced amounts of employee absence
- lower labour turnover (coupled with transient higher turnover among those who do not appreciate or welcome an engagement culture)
- more impressive degrees of organisational citizenship and corporate social responsibility
- enhanced rates of creativity and innovation.

Undoubtedly, the presence of a unifying Big Idea is a crucial starting point for employee engagement, and preferably a Big Idea that embraces all the key dimensions of corporate achievement. Tesco's 'wheel' – its own version of the balanced scorecard – is a sensible starting point, because it encapsulates profitability, customers (spend, loyalty, acquisition and retention), employees (involvement, engagement, commitment and contribution) and change (both proactive and reactive).

Elsewhere, Purcell and his colleagues (2003) have described the features that make a Big Idea meaningful:

- It should be transformationally aspirational rather than merely incremental. In other words, it ought to propose a whole new world for the business rather than the mere extrapolation of existing products/services, customers and profitabilities (or, for non-profit organisations, levels of 'customer' satisfaction).
- The Big Idea should be based on genuine benchmarks and comparators like 'world-class' status and competitive differentiation. The 'world-class' enterprise is one that, by common consent, exhibits superior performance to virtually every other organisation either in its own sector or across the entire sector board.
- The achievement of the aspiration contained within the Big Idea must depend on conscious effort and will not happen naturally. That is why it requires the organisation to orient its corporate, marketing, financial and human resource strategies in a new and energetic direction.
- Realisation of the Big Idea is critically dependent on the contribution of the organisation's people. Nothing will happen without them, because even tangible developments (like new products, new technologies and new processes) are all dependent on the ideas of people through their creativity, their ability to solve problems, their involvement in added-value activities, and their willingness to work with the grain of the business.

Apart from the development of a Big Idea, which itself must be assiduously and consistently promoted from the top down, with no sign of lip-service-paying, no hint of compromise and no cynicism, the organisation also may have to move its structure and *modus operandi*.

If it is a system characterised by a traditional command-and-control hierarchy (and there are still plenty of them around), it will need to move towards a more devolved pattern with centralised management only for the things that have to be managed centrally (i.e. the corporate strategy) and delegated accountabilities for everything else – to separate units, functions, departments, factories, offices and even individual employees. Managing this change is never easy.

 Revolution by devolution

CASE STUDY

Until the 1980s the Halewood car plant on Merseyside was a dark and dirty old factory with grime on the floor and boxes of car parts cluttering the aisles between the production lines. Operators used to eat their sandwiches perched on benches, or would sit in the cars once the seats had been installed.

As *The Economist* (2001) stated, 'Managers used to hide in their offices poring over printouts and emerged on the shopfloor only to shout at workers to get them to do their job better and faster, or even to do it at all, since work tended to interfere with smoking, sleeping, betting or discussing football.'

Not surprisingly, the factory had a history of poor labour relations, and it was therefore surprising to some that when Ford acquired Jaguar they decided to locate production of the then new X-type at Halewood. However, this decision was dependent on a massive culture change coupled with equally massive infrastructure reforms. The assembly area now has a white floor, wide aisles (clearly marked with pedestrian and forklift lanes), large rest areas at intervals with tables and refreshments, plus a noticeboard run principally by the workers themselves.

An orange cord runs at head height all the way along the line. Any operator can pull this to stop the line if they feel it is necessary. In other words, this is a factory designed to be as pleasant as possible to work in and to be micro-managed by the employees. 'In the old days, when we could see a quality issue that needed tackling, we were just ignored,' said one of the Halewood workers. 'Now we are asked to give our

input. Management listens to what we've got to say.'

David Crisp, corporate affairs manager, says: 'We went from a volume-driven culture where you didn't stop the line ever – and that was right through the organisation – to a culture where you stop the line rather than pass on poor quality. But you are trying to change working practices of 30 or 40 years, and you don't just throw a switch and make it happen.' One of the consultants involved in the change process said: 'I talked to a guy in "trim and final" who had stopped the line seven times in eight months. But the first time he did it, he said, "I was shit scared."'

Source: Pickard (2002)

Question

1   In what ways do the changes that occurred at Halewood provide evidence of improved employee engagement?

If the organisation is already decentralised and de-layered, it is psychologically ready for an engagement initiative, and indeed it would be surprising if one had not been launched already, whether formally or otherwise. Then, once the philosophical and physical structures are in place, there have to be associated developments on the HR front, with a special focus on HR planning, recruitment and selection, learning and development, and performance management.

HR PLANNING

Of course, there are many organisations – indeed, a majority – that now decline to participate in any formal HR planning processes, but this shouldn't stop enterprises from setting out a framework of new expectations about employee attitudes, beliefs, behaviours and value-systems. Indeed, such expectations will constitute a self-contained 'Big Idea' for the HR function, although clearly, it's a Big Idea that is derived logically from the very high-level Big Idea that embraces the organisation as a whole.

RECRUITMENT AND SELECTION

Recruitment should be conducted around output- and results-based accountability profiles rather than task-based job descriptions, using company-wide **competency frameworks** rather than role-specific person specifications. Selection systems should heavily emphasise the need for 'fit' between the would-be employee and the organisation's emergent culture. The enterprise must not find itself hampered by people in the workforce who are hostile to change, cynical about employee involvement, and 'disengaged' from the Big Idea.

LEARNING AND DEVELOPMENT

If there hasn't already been a shift from 'training' (what people do to others) to 'learning' (what people do for themselves), such a shift becomes essential. In a high-engagement culture, the need to learn comes from within the learner, and the trainer's role becomes one of facilitation rather than remaining one of instruction. The beauty of this transition, moreover, is that learners actually want to learn, whereas 'trainees' often don't. Another feature of a high-engagement culture is that virtually all its employees are multi-skilled – there is no room for those who might try to claim that anything outside their narrowly vocational training is nothing to do with them. Moreover, the skills model must cover not just lateral skills (job enlargement) but also upward-facing skills such as those traditionally practised by managers, supervisors and team leaders (job enrichment).

PERFORMANCE MANAGEMENT

The high-engagement culture must promote a balance between operational day-to-day achievement (i.e. performing the essential duties associated with the role as defined in the accountability profile or job description) and organisational contribution (i.e. taking part in project teams to resolve remedial issues or create continuous-improvement programmes). Equally, the high-engagement business will not make the mistake of concentrating on too few performance parameters when setting objectives for individuals and departments, because it will know that concentrating on only a few performance parameters will lead to some unintended (and generally undesirable) consequences.

For example, concentrating single-mindedly on sales targets for the customer-facing employees by a retailer of electrical and electronics products will mean that a) customers are neglected if they only want to buy some batteries; and b) customer service is virtually ignored altogether.

We know that in many organisations the business of performance appraisal is not taken seriously. This is not necessarily because the necessary processes don't exist, but rather because managers and executives regard appraisal as a waste of time. Why is that?

● Sometimes it is because the procedures themselves are cumbersome and off-puttingly bureaucratic; they lack credibility because nothing seems to happen after the annual appraisal exercise is finished and also because the system is owned by the HR function.

- Often it is because the system is itself trying to do too much – namely, combine a reward requirement (including pay and bonus) with a personal development focus. Few appraisees are willing to talk about their longer-term personal development when there are short-term and immediate matters (like pay increases and bonuses) to be revealed.
- Frequently it is because managers find it difficult to talk through performance issues with people – and the people with performance issues don't want these issues to be brought out into the open. So there is a kind of conspiracy of silence involving both parties.
- Most commonly it is because the managers who are supposed to lead the appraisal process are not themselves being appraised, so they 'learn' that it can't be important, whatever the organisation may officially prescribe.

None of these barriers to appraisal is inevitable or compulsory. In a high-engagement culture regular appraisal is a constructive process, concerned with employees as 'thinking performers':

- whether they have performed efficiently over the review period, and how both they and their managers working together are going to develop their mutual performance in the future
- whether they have additionally made positive contributions to the business as a whole, and how both they and their managers working together can keep their contributions alive in the future.

To fulfil these aims, the appraisal system must be kept as simple and open-ended as possible. It is even a good idea to call it something other than 'appraisal', since that word has had a bad press in many businesses and it also creates the wrong idea of one person 'appraising' another, instead of the idea that this is an exercise in which people *collaborate* to take themselves (both the appraiser and the appraisee) and the business forward.

Also essential as a factor permeating the entire exercise is that most important of all elements in human relationships – trust. Only if there is a high level of trust in the workforce will those at the top be prepared to delegate decision-making, and only if there is trust in top management will those at the lowest level of the business be prepared to take the risks that are inevitably taken with decisions. In other words, trust is a two-way street. It is especially crucial that people feel able to use their initiative – to act discretionally – without the fear that if they make a mistake they will be punished. Instead, they have to believe that if they do make a mistake (as they undoubtedly will, for every so often anyone who makes decisions will make a poor one, or won't make a decision at all), the mistake will be viewed simply as an opportunity for learning.

The precise mechanisms for establishing trust throughout a business can be notoriously difficult to pin down. Clearly, employees need to have faith in each other, and this is dependent on their experience of working together. As Charles Handy (1995) argued, trust is as fragile as a pane of glass: it takes a long time to make, but can be destroyed in an instant. Employees may trust their managers, but can cease do so immediately if only one manager acts cynically or selfishly, or is judged to have done so.

Critical to creating a climate of trust is the belief among employees that they are partners in a worthwhile psychological contract involving reciprocal obligations between managers and the workforce. Perhaps surprisingly, too, satisfaction with the psychological contract partly depends on the extent to which the employer demonstrates positive attributes as a 'corporate citizen', not just internally but also externally in relationships with the local community.

WHAT ARE THE CONNECTIONS BETWEEN EMPLOYEE ENGAGEMENT AND HIGH-PERFORMANCE WORKING?

It's impossible to discuss employee engagement without reviewing it against the background of another set of currently popular and fashionable concepts associated with high-performance working (HPW). According to the CIPD (2004), 'HPW can be characterised as everything that "Taylorist employment practices" are not.' This may be an unfair comment so far as F. W. Taylor is concerned – especially as his brainchild, 'scientific management', is still practised successfully in some quarters – but what the CIPD is trying to say is that HPW is the

> diametrical opposite of employment strategies based on short cycle times, skill minimisation and 'one right way'.

Such an approach may be appropriate for industries that produce identical goods in very large volumes and which rely on market saturation as the source of their profit margins, but there aren't many of those industries left. Gone are the days when Henry Ford could say, about the Model T car, 'You can have any color you like, provided it's black.' All automotive production lines today are geared up for the idiosyncratic requirements of each individual customer and therefore have to cope with different colours, different transmission systems, different upholsteries, different engine sizes, and even different numbers of cup-holders – all demanded by assertive customers who want exactly what they want and aren't prepared to tolerate compromise.

So this tells us the first thing we need to know about HPW – namely, that it is more suited to product and service sectors that are interested in meeting the needs of their individual customers, often located in different parts of the world where different values, priorities and expectations are held.

HPW places great emphasis on effective people management and indirectly on employee engagement. Unlike simple repetitive work, which can be subject to high levels of control and close supervision, product/service quality in an HPW business is delegated to those who deal directly with customers. Thus an HPW enterprise is characterised by empowerment – decision-making pushed down to the lowest possible level, which generally means to the customer-facing person. It follows, therefore, that an HPW business has relatively little use for supervisors, foremen, chargehands, team leaders or even middle managers, because much of the work previously undertaken by these groups is now performed by operational employees themselves.

It follows that if a business is trying to become an HPW organisation, the strategic, cultural, organisational, developmental and relational implications are likely to be profound. Not all managers are ready to believe that their subordinates can ever be trusted to make sensible choices if allowed to make decisions (e.g. when resolving customer complaints), and not all managers believe that low-level employees could indeed be sufficiently capable to exercise 'discretionary behaviour' options in a way that could productively balance the interests of the business with the interests of the customer.

According to the CIPD (2004), HPW comprises these features:

- a vision based on increasing customer value through differentiating the organisation's products or services and moving towards the customisation of its offering to the needs of individual customers
- a Big Idea, which meets the requirements spelled out by Purcell *et al* (2003):
    - it is *embedded*: solidly rooted in corporate practice
    - it is *connected*: mutually reinforcing both internally and externally
    - it is *enduring*: consistent over time
    - it is *collective*: binding the business together
    - it is *measured and managed*: taken seriously, revisited from time to time to test its continued relevance, and not simply viewed as part of some public-relations corporate rhetoric

- leadership from the top initially and then cascading down through the organisation as necessary in order to create and sustain the HPW momentum, to ensure that the vision and the Big Idea are driven forward
- decentralised and devolved decision-making in which most operational decisions are made by those closest to the customer
- learning as the principal mechanism for enhancing people's capabilities, with a particular emphasis on self-directed learning, self-management, teamworking and project-based activities (e.g. so that cross-functional teams examine issues where remedial action is necessary or look for ways to improve and change)
- performance management processes that are firmly aligned to the organisation's high-level goals – to build trust, enthusiasm and commitment for the business direction
- fair treatment for those leaving the organisation and engagement with the community in the outside world. This may not seem crucial for an HPW enterprise, but in practice it is an important building block for developing trust from the workforce, especially as potential employees these days often want to join companies that have a positive 'social responsibility' profile.

To this list we can add the obligation for strategic people resourcing based on the mantra 'Select for attitude, train for skill'. In other words, an HPW business needs people whose motivational patterns go beyond the instrumental, who are willing to exercise initiative and make decisions, and who are ready to undertake lifelong learning so that they develop and grow with the business instead of staying still while their employer goes forward.

If you find it difficult to remember all the ingredients linked to high-performance working, you might find it easier to distinguish between three separate but interrelated groups of HPW practices:

- high-involvement work practices – e.g. semi-autonomous or autonomous group/ teamworking, job rotation, information-sharing, collective problem-solving and continuous-improvement programmes
- human resource practices – e.g. regular (and meaningful) appraisals, performance management, high levels of training, and so forth
- employee relations practices – e.g. harmonised terms and conditions, joint consultation, team meetings, regular social gatherings for employees, and a strong focus generally on 'employee voice' mechanisms.

WHAT ABOUT THE FUTURE FOR EMPLOYEE ENGAGEMENT?

In reality there is such a close and inseparable connection between employee engagement and high-performance working that for practical purposes the two concepts can be treated as synonymous. It is certainly difficult to visualise any company that has an HPW culture yet has employees who are typically not engaged or who are even actively disengaged; and it is equally difficult to imagine an organisation with high levels of employee engagement yet with no HPW processes or outcomes.

 REFLECTIVE ACTIVITY

1   In what circumstances could an organisation have an HPW culture yet simultaneously experience low levels of employee engagement across its workforce as a whole?

2   In what circumstances could an organisation enjoy high levels of employee engagement yet simultaneously exhibit few if any of the features normally associated with high-performance working?

Think about these two questions, perhaps in relation to the organisation that you work for (or one with which you are familiar).

A few years ago the CIPD and the Engineering Employers' Federation published a joint report (CIPD/EEF, 2003), which reviewed the typical barriers to high-performance working – and therefore, by extension, the barriers to any programmes intended to create high levels of employee engagement.

The report found that companies wishing to introduce HPW must:

- successfully win the trust of their employees
- be prepared to let them become more directly involved in decision-making
- provide extensive training for managers and employees (in the processes and techniques needed if an HPW culture is to take off)
- introduce sophisticated recruitment and selection procedures to ensure that future managers and members of the workforce can support an HPW (and high-engagement) culture.

Furthermore, the success of high-performance working (and employee engagement) depends on a strong, continuous and active commitment from senior management, commitment from employees to the organisation's objectives, the opportunity for both managers and employees to apply discretion to their work, and the pursuit of continuous learning.

Clearly, the future of employee engagement may be particularly problematic in times of economic uncertainty, characterised by high unemployment and fears about the future. Some naïve observers may believe that surely engagement levels will rise as employees thank their lucky stars they still have jobs and work hard to preserve them – but this is not so, for two reasons:

- As we have seen, employees are not truly engaged simply because they are employees: they may still be there, but they could be non-engaged (indifferent) or even actively disengaged (hostile). 'Employment' is not synonymous with 'engagement'.
- People who still have jobs while all around them are losing theirs are inclined to be preoccupied with themselves and their own security – perversely and paradoxically though it may seem, thoughts of engagement are far from their minds.

However, all is not lost. Part of the answer to the problem of creating and sustaining high levels of employee engagement against a background of anxiety and turbulence is to initiate a framework of psychological and social processes that can calm the atmosphere. Nine guidelines developed by Sarah Lewis (2011) are described below.

CREATE A POSITIVE CULTURE

- Actively introduce processes that increase positivity – e.g. by starting meetings with praise for last week's achievements, celebrating successes and creating a work climate of hope and good humour.
- Introduce ways of measuring people's experience of positivity at work, such as asking about positive work experiences in staff surveys.

AFFIRM THE BEST

- Recognise and develop practices that take the business forward reputationally or otherwise.
- Encourage virtuous behaviour such as 'organisational citizenship' and helpfulness to others (e.g. by treating colleagues as customers).
- Regularly recognise team and individual strengths, initiative and innovation, both formally through appraisal processes and informally through MBWA ('management by walking around').

TURN STRENGTHS INTO TALENTS

- When people use their strengths they are more engaged because their self-confidence is much greater.
- Use 'best self-feedback', by which colleagues write accounts of when they have experienced each other at their best.

HELP TEAMS PLAY TO INDIVIDUAL STRENGTHS

- The most productive teams are those where tasks are shared according to the strengths of each individual team member, so encourage team members to swap tasks if in the end a better combination of aptitudes is mobilised.

ADJUST ROLES

- As far as possible, make the job fit the person rather than trying to make the person fit the job; this is much easier if it is acknowledged that most outcomes can be accomplished in different ways.
- Minimise the time staff spend struggling with tasks for which they have no aptitude – or no inclination.

INCREASE 'FLOW'

- 'Flow' is the term used by the American Psychological Association to describe a state of mind in which people become completely involved in an activity and so immersed that they lose all track of time. Flow – and engagement – can result when an employee has job autonomy, support and coaching, feedback, opportunities to learn and develop, task variety and responsibility. It is more likely to occur in particular when the challenge of the work and the person's skill level are well matched.
- Different people experience 'flow' in different ways and from different activities – e.g. becoming absorbed when writing a report, or losing all sense of time when in charge of a training session.
- Find out the sources of 'flow' for people and discover how to increase their opportunities to experience it.

BUILD REWARDS

- Organisations may not have any money to provide financial incentives, but there are plenty of other things that can be rewarding for people, such as praise, appreciation and thanks (particularly if administered publicly, where a sort of multiplier effect comes into play).
- Create a work environment full of small, easily won rewards so that in the end everyone is a winner.

UNDERSTAND GOAL-SEEKING

- People are different, so understanding what makes each person tick is important in order to create goals, milestones and rewards that are immediately relevant.

SUPPORT MEANINGFUL WORK

- People are normally very good at finding meaning in what they do, and we all want to believe we are spending our time valuably.
- Show employees why their work is important, what it means for them, the department, the organisation and even society at large.

- And if nobody can find any meaning in the task, perhaps it's time to review whether the task needs to be done at all.

CONCLUSION

Employee engagement is here to stay. It has a long way to go – not just because there are many organisations that have not yet come to grips with the tools and drivers of engagement, but also because engagement itself is a movable feast. Just as customer aspirations keep rising (there's no imaginable end to them), so the ingredients for employee engagement also keep evolving. Today's high-engagement culture isn't necessarily tomorrow's competitive winner: you have to keep working at it.

What is certain, however, is that the elements listed below will continue to be key to developing, embedding and benefiting from employee engagement.

- a Big Idea – a vision that is ethical, ambitious and ultimately **transformational**, not merely a collection of vacuous platitudes
- coherent, consistent and continuous role-modelling from the top
- good-quality management at all levels – managers who lead, who encourage their teams to perform well, who take an interest in their people and who provide opportunities for development
- two-way open communications – encouragement for 'employee voice' and also keeping employees informed about things that are relevant to them
- collaboration between people, between departments and between functions – a teamworking emphasis that avoids any 'silo' practices and stereotypes
- a customer-centric focus – both customers and people are critical to success
- commitment to employee well-being – taking health and safety seriously, avoiding harassment and discrimination
- a strong, unyielding emphasis on performance and results with challenging and stretching goals that require more than incremental effort
- permanent dissatisfaction with the status quo, coupled with improvement and change programmes
- learning within the organisation and learning from outside – in a high-engagement organisation, the entire workforce is assumed to be a source of 'talent' and the business regularly surveys the outside world to see what can be learned
- clear, accessible HR policies and practices.

 B&Q

CASE STUDY

B&Q was founded in March 1969 in Southampton, by Richard Block and David Quayle. Within 10 years there were 26 stores across the UK, and it subsequently expanded rapidly through a mixture of growth, mergers and acquisitions. It is now owned by parent company Kingfisher plc, and is very active not just in the UK but also in Europe (especially in Poland and France) and further afield. Its store in Beijing is now the largest B&Q store in the world. Today B&Q is the UK's leading do-it-yourself and garden centre retailer and is nearly twice the size of its nearest competitor. It caters for more than 3 million customers a week, through more than 350 stores and with around 23,500 employees.

B&Q was the first retailer in the world, and the only non-US company, to win the Gallup worldwide award for outstanding employee engagement, and has picked up this award every year for the last five years. B&Q has also achieved the *Observer*'s Ethical Business Award, appears on the *Sunday Times* Best Green Companies list and was the first retailer to buy 100% responsibly sourced wood.

Within the context of its Big Idea ('Helping people create homes to be proud of'), B&Q has these five value statements that explain 'how we do things':

● Customer first

● Down to earth

● Respect for people

● We can do it

● Nobody does it better.

These values illustrate what B&Q stands for – both internally and externally. The values are translated into everyday action in various ways. One is by the deliberate recruitment of a diverse workforce because it makes business sense. B&Q customers come from everywhere, so it helps if B&Q employees also come from everywhere.

In 2006 B&Q was one of only two retailers to make *The Times* Top 50 Places Where Women Want To Work, and it has continued this achievement in subsequent years. The company has also acquired a reputation for employing older workers. This was a strategy first tried in 1989 when the company experimentally staffed an entire store (in Macclesfield) with employees over the age of 50. The results were compelling: productivity increased, sales rose and absenteeism fell. Today, over 26% of B&Q employees are over 50, with ages ranging from 16 to 95.

Speaking at a conference in 2003, B&Q's then personnel director, Mike Cutt, claimed that improved levels of employee engagement in B&Q stores could save the company 'tens of millions of pounds' over the next few years. By bringing all B&Q outlets up to the level of its best stores, the company was likely to save around £3 million a year in absenteeism costs, and around £2.5 million a year in recruitment costs. B&Q has also significantly reduced the amount of 'shrinkage' – the loss of stock and profits through employee and customer theft.

The results being achieved at B&Q hold out great hope of an improved status for HR leaders: 'Measuring and quantifying employee engagement is a great opportunity for HR to prove its worth,' said Mike Cutt. 'As a result, we have seen an increase in the training budget at B&Q of around 60 per cent.' This is an aspect of B&Q's personnel and development strategies that has continued to reflect the company's requirement to create an engaged workforce, which will in turn demonstrate a 'world-class people capability'.

The drive towards a significantly improved level of employee engagement received further impetus in 2005, when sales fell by 8 per cent in a single year. Tackling what was regarded as the crucial issue of employee engagement was perceived as essential for the company's recovery, and so B&Q recruited the Gallup Organization, which then administered the Gallup Q12 Index instrument throughout the entire B&Q workforce, including the board, all senior executives and all managers. Everyone was measured on their performance as a leader or manager, and the results published.

They showed that 26% of the company's employees were actively disengaged. At the time, the HR director pointed out that 'We must be a charity – out of a £450 million wage bill, we're spending £120 million on people who don't want to be here. We're paying them to destroy our organisation and make life miserable for all the good, engaged employees.' Some of those who were disengaged were in managerial roles. They were given opportunities to improve, and those who failed to do so, or didn't subscribe to the engagement drive, were asked to leave.

By 2008, the B&Q 'engagement score' (measured by responses to the Gallup Q12 Index instrument) had risen to 60%, compared with a global average of 28% and a UK average of 16%.

Questions

1   B&Q is the only UK retailer to have achieved worldwide recognition for its employee engagement activities. To what extent is it feasible to argue that there are special difficulties in the retail sector so far as employee engagement is concerned?

2   B&Q is well known for its policies about attracting and retaining older workers, and also for its positive reputation for diversity. To what extent might there be a connection between these policies and its employee engagement initiatives?

3   What do you consider to have been the major reasons why the employee engagement score at B&Q has steadily risen over the years since 2005?

FURTHER READING

The MacLeod Report on employee engagement (MacLeod and Clarke, 2009), commissioned by the Department for Business, Innovation and Skills, is available to download free from the Department's website. It provides an excellent and very readable guide to recent research on engagement at work and its potential benefits.

Understanding the People and Performance Link: Unlocking the black box, by John Purcell and his colleagues (2003) deals with issues that go beyond engagement. But it describes a seminal research project that has been very influential on HR practices in this area.

The Towers Watson/Perrin Global Workforce study 2007/2008 (2009) sets out a very coherent and persuasive case for taking employee engagement seriously, also providing good guidance about how it can be enhanced.

REFERENCES

Alfes, K., Truss, C., Soane, E. C., Rees, C. I. and Gatenby, M. (2010) *Creating an Engaged Workforce*. London, Chartered Institute of Personnel and Development.

Buckingham, M. (2001) 'What a waste', *People Management*, 11 October: 19–22.

Churchard, C. (2011) 'Try something new today', *People Management*, 27 January: 19–21.

CIPD (2004) *High-Performance Working*, Factsheet. London, Chartered Institute of Personnel and Development.

CIPD (2009) *Employee Engagement*, Factsheet. London, Chartered Institute of Personnel and Development.

CIPD (2010) *Creating an Engaged Workforce*. London, Chartered Institute of Personnel and Development.

CIPD (2011) *Management Competencies for Enhancing Employee Engagement*. London, Chartered Institute of Personnel and Development.

CIPD/EEF (2003) *Maximising Employee Potential and Business Performance: The role of high-performance working*. London, Chartered Institute of Personnel and Development/EEF.

Development Dimensions International (2006) 'How to … interview for engagement', *People Management*, 26 July.

Fleming, J. H. and Harter, J. K. (2001) 'Optimize', *Gallup Management Journal*, Vol.1, No.4: 14–17.

Handy, C. (1995) 'Trust and the virtual organization', *Harvard Business Review*, Vol.73, No.3: 40–50.

Harter, J. K., Schmidt, F. L. and Hayes, T. L. (2002) 'Business-unit level relationship between employee satisfaction, employee engagement, and business outcomes: a meta-analysis', *Journal of Applied Psychology*, 87: 268–79.

Hutchinson, S. and Purcell, J. (2003) *Bringing Policies to Life: The vital role of front-line managers in people management*. London, Chartered Institute of Personnel and Development.

Kahn, W. A. (1990) 'The psychological conditions of personal engagement and disengagement at work', *Academy of Management Journal*, 33: 692–724.

Lewis, S. (2011) 'How to keep your staff engaged', *People Management*, 13 January: 26.

Lockwood, N. R. (2007) 'Leveraging employee engagement for competitive advantage: HR's strategic role', *HR Magazine* (USA), March: 1–11.

MacLeod, D. and Clarke, N. (2009) *Engaging for Success: Enhancing performance through employee engagement*. A Report to Government. London, Department for Business, Innovation and Skills.

Maitland, R. (2004) 'Engaged tone', *People Management*, 29 January: 52.

Nayar, V. (2010) 'Back to front', *People Management*, 12 August: 26–9.

Patterson, M. G., West, M. A., Lawthorn, R. and Nickell, S. (1997) *The Impact of People Management Practices on Business Performance*. London, Chartered Institute of Personnel and Development.

Pickard, J. (2002) 'Top gear', *People Management*, 18 April: 37–42.

Purcell, J., Hutchinson, S., Kinnie, N., Rayton, B. and Swart, J. (2003) *Understanding the People and Performance Link: Unlocking the black box*. London, Chartered Institute of Personnel and Development.

Robinson, D. and Hayday, S. (2009) *The Engaging Manager*. Brighton, Institute for Employment Studies.

Saks, A. M. (2006) 'The antecedents and consequences of employee engagement', *Journal of Managerial Psychology*, Vol.21, No.7: 600–19.

Salanova, M., Agut, S. and Peiró, J. M. (2005a) 'Linking organisational resources and work engagement to employee performance and customer loyalty: the mediation of service climate', *Journal of Applied Psychology*, 90: 117–22.

Salanova, M., Breso, E. and Schaufeli, W. B. (2005b) 'Hacia un modelo espiral de las creencias de eficacia en el studio del burnout y del engagement', *Ansiedad y Estres* [Anxiety and Stress], Vol.11, No.2/3: 215–31.

Schaufeli, W. B. and Bakker, A. B. (2010) 'The conceptualization and measurement of work engagement', in Bakker, W. B. and Leiter, M. P. (eds) *Work Engagement: A handbook of essential theory and research*. New York, Psychology Press.

Schaufeli, W. B. and Salanova, M. (2007) 'Work engagement: an emerging psychological concept and its implications for organisations', in Gilliland, S. W., Steiner, D. D. and Skarlicki, D. P. (eds) *Research in Social Issues in Management* (Volume 5): *Managing social and ethical issues in organizations*. Charlotte, NC, Information Age.

Schaufeli, W. B., Taris, T. W. and Van Rhenen, W. (2008) 'Alcoholism, burnout and engagement: three of a kind or three different kinds of employee well-being', *Applied Psychology: An International Review*, 57: 173–203.

Towers Perrin (2009) Global Workforce study 2007/2008: 'Closing the engagement gap – a road map for driving superior business performance'. London, Towers Watson.

Xanthopoulou, D., Bakker, A. B., Heuven, E., Demerouti, E. and Schaufeli, W. B. (2008) 'Working in the sky: a diary study on work engagement among flight attendants', *Journal of Occupational Health Psychology*, Vol.13, No.1: 345–56.

CHAPTER 5

Contemporary Developments in Employee Relations

Cecilia Ellis

CHAPTER CONTENTS

- Introduction
- Defining employee relations
- Perspectives on employee relationships
- The parties involved in employee relationships
- The labour market context for employee relationships
- The legal framework for employee relations
- Employee voice practices
- Conflict at work
- Conclusion

KEY LEARNING OUTCOMES

By the end of this chapter, you should be able to:

- explain different perspectives on employee relations

- critically discuss the roles of the government, management and trade unions in employee relations

- analyse the contexts of employee relations and the ways in which they shape relationships between employers and employees

- evaluate the impact of the UK and EU legal framework on employee relations

- evaluate employee voice practices with particular reference to the aims, types and benefits of these practices

• analyse different sources and forms of conflict at work, including approaches to resolving disputes.

INTRODUCTION

Employee relations is traditionally understood to describe the relationship between organisations and trade unions. Although trade unions continue to have an important role to play in employee relations, there are many other features of, and influences on, employee relations in the twenty-first century that merit exploration.

The ways in which employers create and sustain relationships with their employees are complex. These relationships are shaped by the turbulent worlds within and outside of organisations. They are the product of different parties with different interests who hold different levels of power in employee relationships. They are uncertain because there is no guarantee about their duration or outcomes. Contemporary employee relationships are characterised by the need for co-operation, the possibility of conflict and the reality of uncertainty. Managing effective employee relationships is therefore a relevant challenge for HR professionals that demands attention.

This chapter begins by focusing on definitions of and perspectives on employee relations. Then, labour markets are discussed as the world in which employee relationships begin and evolve, and the impact of UK and EU employee law on employee relations is considered. The roles of management, trade unions and government in relation to employee relations are explored, before attention turns to practices and possible outcomes of employee relations. This covers an analysis of employee voice practices, the possibility of conflict at work and approaches to resolving conflict.

DEFINING EMPLOYEE RELATIONS

Before exploring contemporary developments in employee relations, it is important to have an understanding of the nature and characteristics of employee relations. Numerous definitions of employee relations are available, and two main types of definitions can be identified. The first type of definition emphasises the regulatory nature of employee relations, and the second type of definition is relationship-based.

Regulatory-focused definitions of employee relations are exemplified by Gennard and Judge (2010: 225), who claim that 'The purpose of employment relations is to establish rules, regulations and agreements to regulate the employment relationship.' This definition highlights the importance of regulation in employee relations. Regulation of the employee relationship is evident within organisations in staff handbooks, policies and agreements between managers and trade unions collectively (for example, relating to pay) and managers and employees individually (for example, regarding flexible working practices). Regulation of the employee relationship can also occur through sources outside of organisations, in particular when derived from employment law. The government develops laws that regulate the employee relationship (for example, the Equality Act 2010). This regulatory focus can be regarded as a traditional definition of employee relations.

The alternative to the traditional regulatory-focused definition is exemplified by the CIPD Factsheet (2011b), which states that the

> emphasis of employee relations continues to shift from 'collective' institutions, such as trade unions and collective bargaining, to the relationship with individual employees.

These relationships between employers and employees cover the entire employee cycle, from the point at which an employee joins an organisation to the time when they leave an organisation. Whereas this definition recognises that employee relations occur between people, it does not convey the various influences that have an impact on the relationships between employers and employees (for example, the influences of the economic context in the UK and globally on employee relationships).

For the purpose of this chapter, it is suggested that employee relations in contemporary organisations is about creating and sustaining effective employee relationships between employers and employees within the constraints and opportunities presented by organisational contexts. Different ideas about the approaches available to organisations for creating and sustaining relationships are explored in the next section.

PERSPECTIVES ON EMPLOYEE RELATIONSHIPS

The traditional perspectives on employee relationships are derived from the work of Fox in the 1960s. Fox (1966) suggested that there are two main ways in which managers view the employee relationship. One view is described as a **unitarist** relationship, and an alternative view is described as a **pluralist** relationship. Fox (1966) suggested that if managers hold a unitarist view of the employee relationship, they may think of the organisation and workers as a united team who pull together behind the authority of the manager in order to pursue the organisation's goals. An analogy can be drawn between unitarism and a successful football team who support each other on and off the pitch and unite behind the authority of their manager in order to help the football club win matches and increase profits. Unitarist perspectives suggest that the employee relationship is characterised by harmony, co-operation and a team ethic.

An alternative way of thinking about the employee relationship can found in pluralist views. According to Fox (1966), pluralism suggests that organisations and workers have both similar and different interests in the employee relationship. For example, it could be claimed that organisations seek to maximise profits whereas workers seek to develop their careers and maximise their incomes. Although there may be areas of overlap and shared interests, these different agendas can result in tensions and conflict, which must be managed (for example, through discipline and grievance procedures). If a manager holds a pluralist view, conflict is an inevitable feature of the employee relationship, whereas conflict is notably absent from a unitarist view of the employee relationship.

REFLECTIVE ACTIVITY

Two interview candidates are discussing possible responses to interview questions. The candidates are called Katie and Sophie and they both hold CIPD qualifications and have five years' generalist HR experience.

This is an extract from their conversation.

Sophie: The main point that I want to make is that all employees need to be committed to what the organisation is trying to achieve. I know that it can be difficult to get everyone on board but if we communicate the business plans in the right way, people will understand where we are trying to get to and understand how they can contribute so that we all move forward together. Do you think that sounds good?

Katie: Well, I suppose it does sound good if you think it is possible.

Sophie: Of course, everyone needs to pull together. That's what our job is all about isn't it – getting people on board with what the organisation is trying to achieve. Why? Don't you think that's possible?

Katie: Well, if I'm really honest with you, I have my doubts about how realistic it is even though I know it is what senior managers like to hear. I think that people should try to pull together but I don't think it's that easy, especially considering all the different needs and wants

that people bring into an employment situation. Clashes and conflicts are bound to happen, and they need to be managed before we can even think about co-operation.

Sophie: Don't talk to me about conflict. I've had enough of it. That's what I spend all my time dealing with in my current job, and I'm sick of it. That's why I want to move jobs to try and get away from it.

Katie: But do you really think you can get away from it? If you ask me, there's bound to be conflict in employee relationships. I don't think we should ignore it. I think we need to understand that it is inevitable given the different interests of managers and employees. We can add value as HR practitioners by managing the conflict in an appropriate way, which involves being honest about differences and trying to find ways which are mutually acceptable to overcome the differences and work together.

Sophie: Maybe we are talking about the same thing but just approaching it differently?

1   Do you think that Katie and Sophie illustrate unitarist or pluralist perspectives on employee relationships?

2   What are the indicators that suggest their perspectives to you?

Hopefully, the Reflective Activity above enabled you to reflect on the key features of traditional perspectives on employee relationships. In addition to Fox's (1966) unitarist and pluralist perspectives on employee relationships, there are two key alternative views on employee relationships, which highlight features of employee relationships other than conflict. First is the view of employee relationships as an economic exchange in which work is provided in exchange for financial reward. Under this economic view, the employee relationship is all about money – in other words, a financial transaction. For example, an employee who works for money and works harder for more money could be seen as holding an economic view of the employee relationship. This view on the employee relationship has been criticised by some authors as a narrow view of the employee relationship that does not consider the vast array of reasons why people work. Budd (2011: 58), for example, argues that 'work is also undertaken by individuals seeking personal fulfilment and identity', which highlights a limitation of this perspective on employee relationship.

Second is the **psychological contract** view on the employee relationship, which has increased in popularity since the mid-1990s. The CIPD Factsheet on the psychological contract (2011c) defines it as

> the perceptions of the two parties, employee and employer, of what their mutual obligations are towards each other.

This definition suggests that employees perceive that they have obligations to the organisation and that the organisation has obligations towards them. Such perceptions can be concerned with financial aspects of work (e.g. pay) but also other aspects (e.g. career development and job security), which is how this perspective differs from an economic view of the employee relationship. These perceptions that employees and employers hold are seen as important because they define the relationship between employees and employers. If an employee perceives that an employer has met its obligations towards them, the employer may expect some positive effects such as high performance, trust and a willingness to go above and beyond what is required of them by their job description. If, however, an employee perceives that an employer has not met its obligations towards them, the employee can regard their relationship as damaged (referred to as a breach and/or violation in the psychological contract literature) and may expect negative outcomes in the form of reduced levels of performance and turnover. For example, in a redundancy situation, employees may perceive that an organisation has breached its promise to provide them with secure employment and may reduce their performance levels and/or seek alternative employment.

REFLECTIVE ACTIVITY

Imagine that you have been working part-time in a local bar for the last year to help to fund your studies.

1 What are the main things you would expect your manager to do for you?

2 What are the main things that you think that you are expected to do for your manager?

3 If your manager informed you that the business was closing due to falling profits, which, if any, of the above expectations might you think that your manager had breached?

THE PARTIES INVOLVED IN EMPLOYEE RELATIONSHIPS

There are three main parties involved in employee relationships. These are:

- management
- employees and their representatives (trade unions)
- the government.

These parties play different roles, which influence employee relations in various ways. This section analyses the role of each of these parties and its influence on employee relations in contemporary organisations.

MANAGEMENT AND EMPLOYEE RELATIONSHIPS

The term 'management' can be used to refer to a process, a system of authority and a group of people. All of these are relevant in influencing an organisation's employee relations. The process of management includes the organisation and delivery of people and work. Management is a system of authority dependent on the power it holds and exercises through the development and administration of rules. Management can operate individually or as a group of people who hold responsibilities for facilitating the smooth operation of organisations.

Management has a key impact on the day-to-day disposition of employee relationships, and the style that it adopts can determine whether it creates and sustains effective employee relationships. Sisson (2010: 235) argues that since the 1980s, management 'had become the major force for change in the arrangements governing the employee relationship'. This suggests that the role of management in employee relations has increased in comparison with the roles of the government and trade unions.

Management style is the approach adopted by managers in their interactions with employees. Since the 1980s, a number of summaries or typologies of management styles have been produced. A key contribution was provided by Purcell and Sisson (1983), who identified five possible management styles:

- *traditional* – based on the view that management have the right to manage and that employees are a resource to be exploited in order to elicit maximum returns. This management style tends not to welcome trade unions
- *paternalistic* – based on the view that management and employees are part of a team who unite behind the authority of management (i.e. a unitarist view). Paternalistic management style tends to treat employees well and because it is intending to create a united team, does not see the need for input from outside parties such as trade unions
- *consultative* – based on the view that management needs to communicate and consult with employees in order to create and sustain effecting employee relationships. Consultative management style tends to treat employees well and welcomes the contributions of trade unions to the communication and consultation process
- *constitutional* – based on the view that management and employees have some different interests and accept that conflict may feature in employee

relationships (i.e. a pluralist view). Constitutional management style tends to be rule-oriented and regards trade unions as an inevitable part of the management of employee relationships

- *modern* – based on the view that management needs to be flexible in its approach to employee relationships in order to ensure responsiveness to changes. Modern management styles tend to treat employees well and are pragmatic about their relationships with trade unions.

Typologies of management styles, such as that of Purcell and Sisson (1983), can function as a useful tool for managers who want to explore the approaches available to them for managing employee relationships. However, the number of typologies has expanded since the 1980s, which could cause confusion for management seeking to explore its style options. Alternatively, it can be suggested that the numbers of different versions of management styles indicate that a number of different management styles exist and possibly co-exist in contemporary organisations, and that it is possible and perhaps desirable for management to shift between different styles. For example, management style in an organisation that recognises trade unions may be both consultative and constitutionalist. Management can therefore have an impact on employee relationships through its management style and its use of different styles.

Management styles

CASE STUDY

XCo is a market-leading retail business. Last year, XCo achieved record-breaking profits but the workforce is unhappy about how XCo achieved these great results. In particular, employees are concerned about:

- how they have to work seven days a week and have money deducted from their salary if they take time off sick

- the unachievable sales targets, which mean that they rarely achieve their bonuses

- only getting two short breaks during an eight-hour shift and having to ask permission to leave the shop floor to go to the toilet.

The workforce has tried to raise its concerns with management but got the impression that XCo had no intention of changing while it was so profitable, and that if employees felt unable to meet the required standards, perhaps they ought to consider alternative employment.

Questions

1   Using Purcell and Sisson's typology of management style, how would you describe the management style of XCo?

2   What are the advantages and disadvantages of this management style for XCo and the workforce?

3   What alternative management style, if any, might you advise XCo management to consider adopting?

TRADE UNIONS AND EMPLOYEE RELATIONSHIPS

Trade unions are defined in law as 'workers of one or more description and whose principal purposes include the regulation of relations between workers and employers' (Trade Unions and Labour Relations (Consolidation) Act 1992, Section 1). They are independent from government and management but work with those other parties to regulate employee relationships. The largest trade union in the UK is the UNITE union, which had around 1.5 million members in 2010, the members working in a wide range of sectors across the UK.

The role of trade unions is to represent the interests of their members in pursuit of democracy in the workplace. Trade unions can represent their members' interests on an individual basis but rely upon the logic that they can exert more influence on management by operating collectively. They emerged from a desire among working people to re-balance the distribution of power in employee relationships more equally between management and workers. Trade unions have an impact on employee relationships by trying to secure the best possible arrangements for their members, particularly in relation to their salaries. In other words, they seek to enhance the financial and non-financial aspects of the employee relationships of their members. In order to achieve this enhancement, trade unions rely upon heavily upon negotiation and consultation processes. For example, trade unions may negotiate with management about the size of the reward budget available in organisations and then consult with their members before accepting or rejecting a pay deal. In many contemporary organisations, trade unions have been consulting with their members over management proposals to change workers' pension schemes. These proposed changes are the subject of strong resistance from trade unions, who believe that they are unnecessary and detrimental to workers. This example illustrates how trade unions try to have a positive influence on employee relationships for the benefit of their members.

Trade union membership in the UK was at its peak in 1979 when the unions exerted a strong influence on employee relationships. The membership levels of trade unions have been in decline since 1979, as illustrated in Table 5.1.

Table 5.1 Trade union membership levels 1980–2010

Year	Membership (millions)
1980	12.6
1985	10.8
1990	9.8
1995	8.0
2000	7.8
2005	7.5
2010	7.4

Source: Certification Officer's Annual Reports

Table 5.1 illustrates the decline in trade union membership levels and suggests that trade unions have a reduced impact on the management of employee relations in contemporary organisations compared with 30 years ago. Rose (2008) suggests that there are four reasons for the decline in trade union membership levels. These are:

- Employer policies, often influenced by human resource management (HRM), have promoted the individualisation of employee relationships, which runs contrary to the logic of collectivism upon which trade unions rely.
- Membership levels have fallen as unemployment rises in line with business cycles.
- Legislation specifically targeted at reducing the influence of trade unions has led to a drop in membership levels.
- The composition of the workforce has changed. For example, industries such as coalmining and shipbuilding in which union membership levels were high have disappeared. In addition, trade unions have struggled to access members outside of their core membership of male full-time employees (for example, female and temporary workers).

Given the patterns of declining membership levels, the future prospects for trade unions' increasing their influence on employee relationships look limited. In addition to the reasons identified by Rose (2008) for declining membership levels, trade unions have contemporary challenges to overcome in order to increase their impact on employee relations. These challenges include organising on a less UK-centric and more global basis, exploring the possibilities for engaging new and existing members through social media, and attracting and retaining younger members from diverse backgrounds.

REFLECTIVE ACTIVITY

Identify three advantages and three disadvantages for employers and employees of trade union involvement in employee relationships.

THE GOVERNMENT AND EMPLOYEE RELATIONSHIPS

'The government' includes both the current Coalition Government and government agencies such as the Advisory, Conciliation and Arbitration Service (Acas) and the Equality and Human Rights Commission (EHRC) who implement the government's employee policies. The government has a substantial impact on the management of employee relationships through its roles as an employer in the public sector, as a legislator, and through its agencies, which focus on improving the management of problematic areas of employee relationships.

The government can have a direct impact on the management of employee relationships through its roles as employer and legislator. The government is a major employer in the UK owing to the size of the public sector, which includes central and local government and NHS Trusts. This role as an employer provides the government with the opportunity to influence policy and practice through the terms of its employee relationships. Traditionally, the government used this role as employer to demonstrate good practice in employee relations, which led to its being regarded as a model employer. In the model employer era, public sector employee relationships were associated with high levels of job security, pay levels and pension schemes that compared favourably with the private sector and collective employee relationships with an integral role for trade unions.

This model employer tradition has been challenged as different governments (notably Thatcher's Conservative Government of 1979–97) have provided alternative views of what it means to be a model employer. Since 1979, successive governments have sought to increase the efficiency of the public sector and looked to the private sector for inspiration to guide their policies and practices. This has led to the introduction of policies and practices associated with private sector employee relationships – for example, a shift away from promises of a job for life, changes to pension schemes, consideration of the market rate for pay, and the introduction of performance management and individual performance-related pay.

More recently, the Coalition Government's version of what it means to be a model employer has relied upon policies and practices that are designed to achieve substantial cost savings. These include the introduction of job cuts and pay freezes, which have been the source of resistance from employees and trade unions within the public sector. It is clear that these current cost-saving policies and practices will have a significant and direct impact on employee relationships in the public sector during their implementation in 2010–15. What is not clear is whether the government can maintain its traditional role as a model employer during these reforms.

In addition to its role as an employer, the government can also have a direct impact on the management of employee relationships through its role as a legislator. In the UK, the government decides and implements employment laws that originate both from the UK Parliament and from the European Union (EU). There has been a huge growth in employment law over the last 25 years to the point where new legislation is now introduced into the UK on either 6 April or 1 October each year in an attempt to regulate the flow of legislative changes.

When Labour entered government in 1997, the UK signed up to the Social Chapter of the Maastricht Treaty. This committed the UK to adopting a European dimension to its employee policies and practices and to implementing EU law. The European dimension is associated with 'a strong welfare state, a partnership between government, employers and workers, and minimum standards at work' (IRS, 1997). This EU influence is evident in government policies that promote partnership and co-operation between management and trade unions. The implementation of EU law is evident in legislation relating to working hours, the National Minimum Wage and parental leave. These employment laws have substantial implications for reward and flexible working, and illustrate how EU law has a direct impact on UK employee relationships.

The UK government can also exert an indirect influence on employee relationships through its agencies, which include Acas and the EHRC. Acas receives funding from the government but describes itself as an independent body whose aim is to 'improve organisations and working life through better employment relations' (Acas website). In order to achieve this aim, Acas provides advice, information, training and assistance with dispute resolution. For example, the government plans to make more use of Acas' expertise in resolving disputes to try to reduce the number of claims going to employment tribunals. The government announced plans, which will require people to notify Acas if they intend to pursue a claim, and to work with Acas to try to resolve the dispute before making a claim at an employment tribunal. Through these plans, delivered by Acas, the government can influence the process for dispute resolution in the workplace.

The EHRC was formed by the government in 2007 following the merger of three separate specialist equality organisations. The aims of the EHRC are:

● to enforce discrimination legislation

and

● to promote equal opportunities in society.

The government formed this organisation as a vehicle to deliver its equality agenda. In 2010, the Coalition Government committed to eradicate discrimination from workplaces. This commitment is driven by the socially undesirable nature of discrimination, its legally unacceptable nature and the ways in which discrimination is contrary to creating and sustaining effective employee relationships. Through its enforcement and promotion roles, the EHRC can influence the management of employee relationships to achieve the government's equality commitments.

In summary, there are three main parties to employee relationships, and each makes a different contribution to the management of employee relations. Management contributes the organisation's agenda while trade unions contribute the employees' agenda. The government contributes the UK's employee agenda and delivers this directly in the public sector as well as through its legislation and agencies such as Acas and EHRC. The varying agendas of these three parties to employee relationships mean that the management of employee relations is often contested. This contest takes place in the arena of labour markets, which are explored in the next section of this chapter.

THE LABOUR MARKET CONTEXT FOR EMPLOYEE RELATIONSHIPS

Labour markets 'consist of workers who are looking for paid employment and employers who are seeking to fill vacancies' (Claydon and Thompson, 2010: 123). Employee relationships are formed in a marketplace where the product being bought and sold is labour (compared with the goods or services that may be traded in other marketplaces). For employees, the labour market is the place where they search for a job. For employers, the labour market is the place where they look for and find someone to do a job for their organisation. However, it is misleading just to think about a single labour market because there are many different types of labour markets for different skills in different locations within which employee relationships are formed.

Let us imagine that you are already working for an organisation but want to develop your career further. You might start by considering job opportunities within your current organisation. This is an example of an *internal* labour market. If your current organisation did not have any suitable vacancies for you to apply for, you might search for job opportunities outside of your organisation in the *external* labour market. Then, in the external labour market, if you are a graduate, you might search for jobs mainly in the *graduate* labour market. Once you have gained sufficient experience in a graduate role, you might thereafter search for job opportunities within *local, national or international* labour markets. Similarly, if you are an employer, depending on the type of vacancy that you have in your organisation, you may search for employees in the *internal* and/or *external* labour markets.

Like all marketplaces, labour markets are affected by the forces of demand and supply. A shop is an example of a marketplace, and is affected by the numbers of customers who want to buy their goods (*demand*) and the amount of goods they stock for sale in their shop (*supply*). Labour markets are affected by the numbers and types of people who are searching for jobs and the numbers and types of vacancies that exist. The *demand* for labour relates to the numbers and types of vacancies that employers are seeking to fill. The *supply* of labour relates to the numbers and types of people who are searching for work. It is rare that the demand for, and supply of, labour, are equal. More frequently, it can be observed that there are more vacancies in labour markets than they are people suitable to fill them (a situation where demand exceeds supply). The likely outcome of this imbalance between demand and supply is a shortage of people and particular skills. Or alternatively, there may be more people searching for jobs than there are vacancies for them to fill (a situation where supply exceeds demand). The likely outcome of this imbalance between supply and demand is unemployment.

Considering the supply side of labour markets in more depth, the workforce can be divided into three categories: employed people, unemployed people and economically inactive people (which includes full-time students, carers and disabled people). Table 5.2 illustrates the numbers of people in each of these categories in the UK in 2011.

Table 5.2 The size of categories of the UK workforce

Category	Numbers of people in the UK (millions)	Percentage
Employed	29.07	70.2
Unemployed	2.62	8.3
Economically inactive	9.36	23.3

Source: Labour Market Statistics, November 2011

Table 5.2 informs us that the majority of the workforce are in the employed category. The size of the employed category has been boosted by the increasing numbers of women in the workplace as it has become more socially acceptable for women to work. This increasing feminisation of the workplace has altered the gender basis of labour markets from being male-dominated to being more diverse. The size of the unemployed category has varied according to economic climates. According to the Office for National Statistics, current levels of unemployment are at their highest for 16 years, which suggests that supply of labour exceeds demand for labour.

Table 5.2 does not, however, provide insights into the skills and educational profile of the workforce, which might mean that there are skills that are in short supply. In 2006, a review of the UK skills base was undertaken by Lord Leitch. The review found that the UK's skills base was weak in comparison with other international competitors', a finding, which suggests that the current composition of labour markets includes a low skills base. The Leitch Review also found that one out of every six people is defined as illiterate or innumerate, which suggests that high levels of skills and education are in short supply in labour markets – which limits the ability of the UK to compete with countries such as the USA, Canada and Germany, which have a stronger skills base.

Turning to the demand side of labour markets, the decline of industries including coalmining and shipbuilding has contributed to a shift in demand for employment from manufacturing to the service sector. This has reduced the demand for manual employment and increased the demand for managerial and professional employment. Such an increase in demand for managerial and professional employment may be at odds with the low levels of skills and education identified by the Leitch Review. It may also contribute to a division in labour markets between high skill/high pay employment and low skill/low pay employment. The concern about this possible division is that it reduces the middle ground of employment with mid-range skill/mid-range pay, which may be achievable and desirable for large numbers of the workforce.

The public sector is often associated with high levels of demand for mid-range skill/mid-range pay employment. During the Labour Government between 1997 and 2010, large numbers of jobs were created in the NHS, education, local government and the police. This meant that the composition of employment in labour markets could be more evenly balanced between high, medium and low ranges of skill and pay. However, the Coalition Government's comprehensive spending review in 2010 announced substantial job losses in the public sector, meaning that there will be less demand for public sector workers between 2010 and 2015. The government's intention is that this decline in demand will be compensated for by growth in the private sector and job creation such as the announcement by GlaxoSmithKline in March 2012 of plans to build a new factory in Ulverston, Cumbria, which is expected to create 1,000 jobs. Without such job creation, however, there is a possibility of a more pronounced division in labour markets between the higher and lower ranges of skill and pay.

Such problems may prompt action from the government through the introduction of laws and policies. Government regulation may seek to respond to particular problems such as unemployment and skills shortages or may be designed to promote its twin goals for labour markets, which are employability and flexibility. Employability is frequently pursued by universities, who seek to prepare their students both academically and practically with the knowledge and skills to enter and develop in employment. Flexibility is frequently pursued by employers, who want to be able to respond in a competitive global market that is increasingly high-tech and turbulent.

In order to pursue its goal of employability, the government promotes apprenticeships and work experience schemes designed to encourage young people into labour markets. Such schemes are not always received positively. For example, the government's work experience schemes were criticised in 2012 for 'exploiting' young workers. There are also some potential barriers to the achieving of employability goals for labour markets highlighted by the Browne Review of higher education.

This Review aims to transfer the costs of higher education from the government to students while endeavouring at the same time to improve the quality of the student experience. The government claims that by lifting restrictions on tuition fees and effectively deregulating the higher education market, it is encouraging competition between universities, which is intended to raise the quality of the student experience. However, whether or not these reforms will contribute to the government's goal of employability is debatable because the rising costs of tuition fees could deter students from accessing higher education. Current evidence suggests the possibility of a small reduction in demand for higher education. This could have long-term implications for graduate labour markets. If the supply of graduates diminishes owing to the rising costs of university education, there is a possibility that the demand for talented graduates will exceed the supply, leading to a shortage of these people. Although this Review may meet its aims of reducing government expenditure on higher education, it may not directly advance the government's focus on employability.

The pursuit of labour market flexibility by the government has provided employers with flexibility to change the size, composition and deployment of their workforce in line with changing demands. For example, employers have the flexibility to ask employees to agree to work longer than their usual weekly hours in order to respond to an unexpected increase in demand. The government's goal of labour market flexibility has provided employees with opportunities for work–life balance. For example, employees can require employers to give serious consideration to their requests to work part-time. Although this aspect of flexibility may be desirable for some employees, some employers may argue that it is not feasible for their employees to work part-time. Furthermore, the pursuit of flexibility is regarded as incompatible with long-term job security. This has contributed to a shift away from employers promising a job for life in the changing marketplaces in which they may operate, which can make long-term security of employment rare. Although this may be desirable for the government and for some employers, this consequence of labour market flexibility may not be desirable for employees, who may view the more insecure nature of employment as a source of anxiety. So although the purpose of labour market regulation may appear to be logical, the regulatory practices are complicated and can be controversial.

What, then, are the implications of these contemporary trends in labour markets for employee relationships? Labour markets are the changing worlds within which employee relationships are created and sustained. Labour markets are varied and complex in nature, which implies the need to think of a range of forms of employee relationships that exist in current labour markets. These include employee relationships of a long- and short-term nature, and those of a typical and atypical nature. The complexities of labour market regulation mean that policies and practices that are introduced into employee relationships may have mixed effects for employers and employees and could be a source of conflict in the employee relationship. The trends in labour markets towards increasing demand for higher-skilled managerial employment may be inconsistent with the skills base of the UK workforce, which may not be able to supply what is required. The impact of recent policies such as the Browne Review on higher education could exacerbate this shortfall and mean that organisations face particular challenges in creating and sustaining employee relationships that will contribute to the enhancement of the UK's skills base.

THE LEGAL FRAMEWORK FOR EMPLOYEE RELATIONS

Employee relationships are shaped and influenced by a legal framework. This legal framework is designed to promote particular behaviours (for example, work–life balance) and to regulate management behaviour towards employees (for example, protecting employees from harassment). There has been a substantial growth in the legal regulation of employee relationships over the last 40 years, which means that employment law plays a key part in the management of individual and collective employee relationships. For those involved in the management of employee relationships, ensuring legal compliance is essential.

The legal framework is evident in employee relationships in the form of contracts of employment. In contrast to a *psychological contract*, which is about employees' expectations, a *contract of employment* is a legally enforceable agreement between an organisation and an employee. It is formed after an organisation makes an offer of employment to an employee, the employee accepts that offer, and then begins to work in exchange for reward. The idea of a contract of employment as an exchange between employers and employees has some critics, who argue that the exchange between employers and employees is inherently unfair. This is based on the view that employers hold the balance of power in employment relationships and are therefore in a position to determine the terms of the exchange whereas employees hold a subordinate position and are effectively bound to accept the terms offered to them by employers.

Notwithstanding debates on the fairness of the formation of contracts of employment, the content of contracts of employment can either be expressly agreed terms or implied terms. Express terms are explicitly agreed between employers and employees, outline the rights and obligations of both parties, and typically cover the following areas:

- job title
- rate of pay
- when and how payment is to be made
- start date
- hours of work
- place of work
- holiday entitlement/pay
- pension provision
- sickness absence
- notice requirements.

Implied terms, on the other hand, are details that can be inferred as included within contracts of employment. Mutual trust and confidence is an example of an implied term. It is not usually expressly stated within contracts of employment, but it is generally accepted that it is an essential feature of employee relationships. If an employer cannot trust its employee to do his or her job to a good standard without constant direct supervision, the future of their relationship is limited. If an employee does not trust the employer to pay him or her on a regular basis, the employee may not be able to afford to continue with this employment. Implied terms may provide employees and employers with rights and obligations depending on the circumstances. In the case of mutual trust and confidence, it is usual to consider this implied term as incorporated within contracts, but if other implied terms are unusual, they may not be so incorporated into contracts of employment. If the content of a contract of employment is breached by employers or employees, the other party can seek remedies for such a breach. Remedies are frequently financial – and this highlights the consequences of not managing (and the incentives to manage) employee relationships within the legal framework.

Keeping up to date with the changing legal framework is a challenge for managers and HR professionals. The legal framework is subject to change through new legislation and amendments to existing legislation emerging from both UK and EU institutions on a regular basis. In the UK, the main source of employment law is legislation or Acts of Parliament. These become law once they are approved by the Houses of Parliament and the sovereign. Recent examples of such legislation are the Employment Acts of 2002 and 2008, which cover areas including procedures for resolving disputes between employers and employees.

In addition to legislation, other sources of employment law include common law and Codes of Practice. Common law is made by judges based on decisions reached on cases considered in the courts. These decisions set precedents or benchmarks, which can be applied to similar cases. For example, there can be uncertainty about whether someone is an employee, and this has implications for his or her ability to make employee tribunal claims against the employer. Over time, a series of tests have been developed by judges hearing similar cases, which are intended to help other judges thereafter reach a decision on employee status.

Such tests can be applied in the context of each case to inform decisions. Codes of Practice do not have legal status but they provide guidance on laws and are expected to be used in the management of employee relationships. For example, the Acas Code of Practice on Discipline at Work outlines the steps that employers and employees are expected to take to ensure the effective handling of disciplinary cases, and is an example of how the legal framework can have a direct impact on employee relationships.

European law has informed UK employment law since the UK joined the European Community in 1973. There are various forms of European law including Regulations and Directives, Regulations being the most important type of EU legislation (for example, the Working Time Regulations). Regulations and Directives are developed in the EU and then implemented in the UK. There has been a notable growth in the EU as a source of law since Labour signed up to the Social Chapter in 1997, leading to legislation in the UK including that relating to the transfer of undertakings, information and consultation, part-time work, agency workers and fixed-term contracts. This source of employment law has contributed a European dimension to the management of employee relationships.

Key developments in employment law can be broadly categorised into individual and collective laws. Individual developments relate to laws regulating employee relationships, whereas collective developments apply to laws regulating relationships between employers and trade unions, and trade unions and their members. In the area of individual laws, four key developments are summarised below.

- the Equality Act 2010
- The Equality Act 2010 consolidates and reviews a raft of existing discrimination laws and specifically aims to achieve equality of pay between men and women. The impact of this Act on employee relationships is likely to be minimal because there are limited changes included in the Act. Instead, the Equality Act 2010 may encourage employers to enhance their existing approaches to ensuring equality in employee relationships.
- default retirement age (2011)
- The default retirement age of 65 was removed in 2011, and means that employers can no longer require employees to retire at age 65. Employees can continue to work for longer than previously, with no specific end date for employee relationships. This is evident at organisations such as B&Q, who have sought to recruit more mature workers, and potentially increases the open-ended and uncertain nature of employee relationships.
- the Agency Workers Regulations 2010
- The Agency Workers Regulations 2010 mean that temporary agency workers are now eligible for the same treatment as permanent employees. It is intended to provide employees in a precarious position with more rights and protections. This blurs the distinction between permanent and temporary employees, and has the effect of standardising employee relationships and potentially reducing the demand for temporary workers.
- an increase in qualifying service for unfair dismissal (2012)

- In April 2012, the qualifying service required by employees in order to lodge a claim for unfair dismissal at an employee tribunal increased from 12 months to two years. This was intended to reduce the numbers of claims made to employee tribunals and to provide employers with more flexibility to recruit and dismiss employees based on their business needs. It can be argued that it provides employers and employees with more time to create and sustain effective employee relationships. However, the change reduces the protection for employees against being unfairly dismissed and means that employee relationships could become more insecure for employees until they accrue two years' continuous employment.

The main developments in the area of collective law relate to information and consultation provisions, trade union recognition and restrictions on industrial action, as summarised below.

- the Information and Consultation of Employees (ICE) Regulations 2004
- The ICE Regulations were introduced to promote meaningful information and consultation arrangements. In particular, the Regulations require employers to inform and consult with employees and/or their representatives about the likelihood of any business changes that might affect job security. The Regulations offer the potential for employees to be better informed about and consulted upon key business decisions, such as redundancy. However, in practice, the Regulations can be interpreted loosely by employers, meaning that employees can be involved in exchanges of information about business performance and can be involved in consultation exercises over the future plans for a business, but may remain not necessarily any better informed nor able to influence future business plans. These Regulations have not therefore definitively improved the arrangements for information and consultation in employee relationships.
- statutory trade union recognition (2000)
- The Employment Relations Act 1999 means that employers are legally bound to recognise a trade union if the majority of employees vote in favour of trade union recognition. Once a union is recognised, employers have to negotiate with trade union representatives to determine pay and possibly hours of work and holiday entitlements. This recognition introduces a collective flavour to employee relationships, which requires employers and trade unions to jointly regulate employee relationships – which in turn implies some power-sharing between management and trade unions. Potentially, statutory trade union recognition can increase the influence of trade unions on employee relationships. Although reasonably high numbers of trade union recognition agreements have been signed, however, there is no indication of a halt in the overall decline of trade union membership levels. This suggests that trade unions may contribute to the regulation of many employee relationships but that statutory recognition has not necessarily increased the influence of trade unions on employee relationships.
- industrial action
- Although it is not the subject of new developments, the law on industrial action has been highlighted in the last five years through a small number of high-profile strikes, such as the British Airways dispute. Unlike other countries in the

European Union, there is no legal right to strike in the UK, and strike action is regarded as undesirable by management and a last resort for trade unions and their members. In order for trade unions and their members to take lawful strike action, a lengthy ballot process must be followed. This requires trade unions to be highly organised and can act as a deterrent to strike action. It also provides employers with time to challenge the planned strike action, to try to resolve the dispute, and to plan for any disruption that may occur during a strike. In the case of the British Airways cabin crew dispute, a flaw in the ballot process adopted by the trade union enabled the management of British Airways to avert a strike planned for Christmas 2009. Notwithstanding the flaws in the ballot process, the British Airways dispute reminds us that employees have a voice – and the different voice practices used in contemporary organisations are explored in the next section.

REFLECTIVE ACTIVITY

In what ways has the UK and EU legal context had an impact in your workplace (or one with which you are familiar)?

EMPLOYEE VOICE PRACTICES

Employee involvement and participation are forms of employee voice which, according to Benson and Brown (2010: 83),

> provide employees with the opportunity to express their concerns and to influence the actions of management.

Employee voice is traditionally associated with trade unions on the view that employee voice has to be channelled through trade union representation in order to have any impact. However, in the light of the decline in trade union membership levels, it can no longer be assumed that forms of employee voice will involve trade union input, and that where they do, trade union involvement will enhance the impact of employee voice. Instead, there has been a growth in non-trade-union forms of employee voice by which there is direct communication between management and employees on an individual and/or collective basis without any input from a third-party trade union representative.

There are two main forms of employee voice. First, there is **employee participation**, which is where employees participate in organisational decision-making through their representatives. Examples of employee participation practices include partnership working, joint consultation committees and employee forums. Employee participation can be contrasted with **employee involvement**, which is where management introduces practices directly with employees in order to gain their ideas and co-operation. Examples of employee involvement practices include email communications, management briefings, problem-solving groups, suggestion schemes and newsletters. Based on data from the Workplace Employment Relations Survey (WERS, 2006), it is apparent that downward communication is the most extensively used form of employee voice in contemporary organisations. This is interesting because it constitutes a direct form of communication that does not involve trade unions and exemplifies a growth in non-trade-union forms of voice.

The use of employee voice practices was optional for organisations until 2005 when the Information and Consultation of Employees (ICE) Regulations were implemented in the UK. These Regulations provided employees with a legal right to be informed and consulted with about various employee matters, notably the likelihood of any changes to employee relationships and job security. As well as providing organisations with legal compliance, employee voice practices are believed to have benefits for both employers and employees. According to the CIPD (2011b), the benefits for employers are regarded to be:

- employees' skills and knowledge can be better used, leading to higher productivity
- employees feel more valued, so they are more likely to stay and to contribute more
- the organisation gains a positive reputation, making it easier to recruit good employees
- conflict is reduced and co-operation between employer and employee is based on interdependence.

The CIPD (2011b) highlights the following benefits of voice practices for employees:

- having more influence over their work
- higher job satisfaction
- more opportunity to develop skills
- more job security if their employer is more successful as a result of 'voice initiatives'.

This suggests that as well as being a legally essential feature of employee relationships, employee voice practices can be beneficial to both employers and employees. However, research by Marchington and Wilkinson (2005) suggests that different employee voice practices can have different levels of impact. They argue that voice practices can be evaluated based on factors including their depth and scope. They believe that some voice practices are of deeper importance and are concerned with a broader range of issues than others, which enables employees to have more of an influence on organisational decision-making. For example, they regard practices that provide employees with information as being shallow in depth and narrow in scope, and therefore providing employees with limited opportunities to influence organisational decision-making. In contrast, they evaluate practices that involve consulting with employees and/or their representatives as being of deeper importance and broader scope. This suggests that different employee voice mechanisms have different outcomes and offer employees varying levels of influence and opportunity to contribute to organisational decision-making. Although downward communication has grown in popularity, this employee involvement practice can be evaluated as shallow in depth and narrow in scope, which may limit the power and influence of this type of voice.

In summary, employee voice practices are an essential feature of employee relationships. There are different forms of employee voice practices, and each form has advantages and disadvantages for employers and employees and their representatives. There has been a growth in non-trade-union forms of employee voice, but there are doubts about the impact of these practices.

CONFLICT AT WORK

In line with a pluralist view of employee relationships, conflict is regarded as inevitable owing to the different interests of parties to employee relationships. What is important for organisations under this approach is to ensure that they have robust systems in place to manage conflict. In contrast, a unitarist view of employee relationships assumes that conflict will not occur owing to the alignment of management and employee interests. Conflict is regarded as the exception rather than the norm under a unitarist approach.

According to Sisson (2010: 207),

Conflict, which can be defined as the discontent arising from a perceived clash of interests, can involve individuals and/or groups and take a number of expressions.

Table 5.3 summarises the different forms of conflict that can be evident in contemporary organisations.

Table 5.3 Different forms of conflict

Organised conflict	Unorganised conflict
Strikes	Fiddles/theft
Protests, demonstrations, boycotts	Sabotage
Work-to-rule, go-slow, overtime bans	Absence, resignation

Source: Williams and Adam-Smith (2010: 343)

Organised conflict – such as strikes – usually occurs on a collective basis. An example of this type of conflict was evident on 30 November 2011, when thousands of public sector employees took strike action in protest at the government's proposed changes to pension arrangements. Organised conflict can be official if it has been organised by a trade union, or unofficial if it has not been formally approved by a trade union. There is an expectation that conflict organised by trade unions will be lawful through compliance with the legal framework outlined in TULRCA (1992). Unofficial organised conflict tends to be unlawful although frequently short-term (for example, a group of employees may instigate a go-slow for part of a working day in order to demonstrate their discontent, before returning to normal working practices). In Table 5.3, organised conflict is distinguished from unorganised conflict, or 'misbehaviour' as it is sometimes known. Misbehaviour such as sabotage can occur on an individual and/or collective basis. For example, if an individual or group of employees is dissatisfied with an organisation's decision to make employees redundant, they could damage property belonging to the organisation as an expression of their discontent.

Conflict at work is traditionally associated with strikes. However, in contemporary organisations, this association is misconceived. Statistics on strike action illustrate that strikes have declined in the UK. At their peak in 1979 there were 29.4 million working days lost from strike action, compared with 1.39 million working days lost from strike action during 2011 (Labour Market Statistics, February 2012). A number of reasons have been suggested for the decline in strike action, including the impact of a decline in trade union membership levels over the same period and an increasingly complex legal framework, both of which can be regarded as making it harder for trade unions to conduct lawful and significant strike action. It is plausible to predict an increase in the numbers of days lost from strike action during the implementation of austerity measures in the public sector from 2010 to 2015. It is, however, highly unlikely that any increase will herald a return to the high levels of the 1970s given the deterrents, costs and limited public support for strike action.

In contemporary organisations, conflict is more associated with individual than with collective forms, expressed as grievances, absence, resignations and complaints to employment tribunals. The CIPD's (2011a) Conflict Management survey reported that there had been an increase in the mean (average) numbers of grievance per organisation each year from 8 in 2007 to 22.3 in 2011. Data from the Employment Tribunals Service indicates an increase in numbers of employment tribunal claims between 2008/9 and 2009/10, as illustrated in Table 5.4.

Table 5.4 Total numbers of claims made to employment tribunals

Year	Number of claims
2008/9	151,028
2009/10	236,100
2010/11	218,100

Source: Annual Tribunal Statistics, 1 April 2010 to 31 March 2011

The growth in numbers of employment tribunal claims between 2008/9 and 2009/10 prompted the government to issue proposals for the reform of the employment tribunal system in an attempt to reduce the numbers of claims. For example, the government plans to increase the qualifying length of service for claiming unfair dismissal from one to two years. This change is intended to reduce the numbers of claims – but whether or not these reforms will reverse the contemporary trend towards the use of employment tribunals as an expression of individual dissatisfaction remains to be seen.

Conflict of whatever form can be regarded as having undesirable effects on employee relationships. Even if managers adopt a pluralist view that conflict is inevitable, there remains a desire to resolve disputes in order to minimise any detrimental impacts on performance, working relationships and organisational reputation. The CIPD's Conflict Management survey (2011a) indicates that organisations have increased their investment in training managers to help with conflict resolution, specifically offering help with handling difficult conversations. Although this is an essential skill that may enable managers to resolve disputes more effectively, there is also a need for managers to be aware of and compliant with the legal framework that governs the handling of discipline and grievance cases. Furthermore, the point at which managers are facing difficult conversations may be too late to prevent conflict escalating into strikes or employment tribunal claims. In view of the key role of managers in conflict management, therefore, there is a case for broader investment in supporting managers with conflict prevention and resolution to complement any training provided in dealing with difficult conversations.

The CIPD's Conflict Management survey (2011a) reveals that 85% of disciplinary and grievance cases are resolved internally within organisations. However, if all internal options for resolving disputes have been exhausted, organisations can draw upon the services of independent organisations such as Acas to assist with dispute resolution. Acas can assist organisations to resolve disputes through the use of arbitration, conciliation and **mediation** techniques. Arbitration is an option for resolving disputes relating to unfair dismissal and flexible working by which an independent person (an arbitrator) evaluates the dispute and issues a binding decision. Conciliation attempts to identify a mutually acceptable resolution to a dispute that has resulted or is likely to result in a claim to an employment tribunal. Mediation is essentially the same as conciliation, except that the dispute has not resulted in an employment tribunal claim. Acas identifies mediation as the most commonly appropriate form of conflict resolution, and the technique is likely to broaden as a result of government proposals that highlight the importance of mediation for resolving disputes.

In summary, various forms of conflict are evident in organisations owing to the different interests of the parties to employee relationships. This undermines the achievability of a unitarist approach to employee relations. In contemporary organisations, conflict is more likely to manifest itself in individual forms such as grievances and employment tribunal claims rather than collective forms, including strikes. This creates challenges for creating and sustaining effective employee relationships amid the possibility of conflict.

CONCLUSION

This chapter has highlighted the key features of employee relationships in contemporary organisations. The chapter began by defining employee relationships as the main focus of employee relations and discussed different perspectives on employee relationships. Next, the contribution of management, trade unions and government to the management of employee relationships was explored, the influences of labour market contexts were discussed, and the legal framework on employee relationships was examined. Finally, the practices of employee voice and the realities of conflict at work were analysed.

Looking ahead, it is reasonable to suggest that the business of creating and sustaining employee relationships will continue to be relevant and extremely important over the next five years. The reforms of higher education, the promotion of apprenticeships and the removal of the default retirement age may create more entry and exit points into and out of labour markets, meaning that employee relationships are likely to expand in overall duration. However, in order to maintain and possibly enhance the skills base of the UK, the government and organisations may be required to invest more heavily in their training and development provision, including the apprenticeship scheme, or look outside the UK in order to meet skills gaps. This will involve investment in employee relationships, which may be difficult for some organisations without a secure economic position.

The decline in trade union membership shows no signs of abating, which suggests that the role of trade unions in the management of employee relationships will continue to diminish. In line with this decline, the growth of employee involvement rather than employee participation forms of employee voice may be expected to continue. There is, however, an opportunity for the trade union movement to engage with the mediation agenda in the area of dispute resolution and to demonstrate different ways of thinking and acting through its involvement in the public sector reforms. Because the public sector is likely to shrink in size and bear a closer resemblance to the private sector with an emphasis on competition, resistance and conflict are likely. This presents a longer-term challenge for managers and HR practitioners in balancing the need for co-operation with the expectation of conflict, amid the continuing reality of uncertainty.

FURTHER READING

Acas (2011) *The Future of Workplace Relations – An Acas view*. [Online] Available at: http://www.acas.org.uk/media/pdf/n/8/The_Future_ of_Workplace_Relations_-_An_Acas_view.pdf. This report provides some predictions about the future directions for employee relations over the next ten years.

CIPD (2005) *What is Employee Relations?* [Online] Available at: http://www.cipd.co.uk/hr-resources/research/employee-relations.aspx. This report outlined the contemporary focus on employee relations, and prompted debate among academics and practitioners about the changing nature and relevance of employee relations.

CIPD (2011) *Employee Relations at capgemini UK*. [Online] Available at: http://www.cipd.co.uk/hr-resources/research/employee-relations-capgemini-uk.aspx. This is an interesting case study, which explores contemporary employee relations practices within the context of a global IT services organisation.

CIPD (2012) *Employee Relations* Information Page. [Online] Available at: http://www.cipd.co.uk/hr topics/employee-relations.aspx. This website provides factsheets, podcasts and survey reports on the subject of employee relations.

Gennard, J. and Judge, G. (2010) *Managing Employment Relations*, 5th edition. London, Chartered Institute of Personnel and Development. This CIPD text discusses the contexts of employee relations, explores key theoretical perspectives and discusses employee relations practices in depth.

Lewis, P., Thornhill, A. and Saunders, M. (2003) *Employee Relations: Understanding the employment relationship*. Harlow, Pearson Education. This text focuses on the employee relationship as the central feature of employee relations and provides a comprehensive overview of key areas with practical examples to consolidate learning.

Rose, E. (2008) *Employment Relations*, 3rd edition. Harlow, Pearson Education. This is a useful resource, which provides a comprehensive overview of the theory and practices of employee relations.

REFERENCES

Benson, J. and Brown, M. (2010) 'Employee voice: does union membership matter?', *Human Resource Management Journal*, Vol.20, No.1: 80–99.

Budd, J. W. (2011) *The Thought of Work*. New York: Cornell University Press.

CIPD (2011a) *Conflict Management survey*. London, Chartered Institute of Personnel and Development.

CIPD (2011b) *Employee Relations*. Overview Factsheet. July. London, Chartered Institute of Personnel and Development.

CIPD (2011c) *The Psychological Contract*, Factsheet. London, Chartered Institute of Personnel and Development.

Claydon, T. and Thompson, A. (2010) 'Human resource management and the labour market', in Beardwell, J. and Claydon, T. (eds) *Human Resource Management: A contemporary approach*, 6th edition. Harlow, FT/Prentice Hall.

Fox, A. (1966) 'Industrial sociology and industrial relations', Donovan Commission Research Report, No. 3. London, HMSO.

Gennard, J. and Judge, G. (2010) *Managing Employment Relations*, 5th edition. London, Chartered Institute of Personnel and Development.

Kersley, B., Alpin, C., Forth, J., Bryson, A., Bewley, H., Dix, G. and Oxenbridge, S. (2006) *Inside the Workplace: Findings from the 2004 Workplace Employment Relations Survey*. Abingdon, Routledge.

Leitch, S. (2006) 'Prosperity for all in the global economy – world class skills'. Final Report. The Leitch Review of Skills. London, HM Treasury.

Marchington, M. and Wilkinson, A. (2005) 'Direct participation', in Back, S. (ed.) *Personnel Management: A comprehensive guide to theory and practice*, 4th edition. Oxford, Blackwell.

Purcell, J. and Sisson, K. (1983) 'Strategies and practices in industrial relations', in Bain, G. S. (ed.) *Industrial Relations in Britain*. Oxford, Blackwell.

Rose, E. (2008) *Employment Relations*, 3rd edition. Harlow, Pearson Education.

Sisson, K. (2010) *Employment Relations Matters*. Available at: www2.warwick.ac.uk/ fac/soc/wbs/research/irru/.

Williams, S. and Adam-Smith, D. (2010) *Contemporary Employment Relations: A critical introduction*, 2nd edition. Oxford, Oxford University Press.

CHAPTER 6

Reward Management

Graham Perkins and Carol Woodhams

CHAPTER CONTENTS

KEY LEARNING OUTCOMES

By the end of this chapter, you should be able to:

- analyse the context of reward management, highlighting key internal and external factors that influence reward processes and systems

- critically discuss the most appropriate methods of gathering and analysing data relating to reward management

- analyse the various theories and perspectives that underpin the reward management field

- evaluate the concept of 'total reward', highlighting its overall aims and key benefits

- analyse various reward management practices, including grade/pay structures, job evaluation and the idea of 'contingent reward'

- critically discuss the role that line managers play in reward management systems and processes.

INTRODUCTION

When **reward management** is discussed and analysed within organisations, cash pay is often the first thing that comes to mind. It is very important to remember that cash pay is only one part of reward management and that there are many other factors and variables that must be considered.

The way in which employees are rewarded can provoke a great deal of controversy both within and outside organisations. The methods and reasons that sit behind reward decisions have strategic, practical and symbolic implications, so it is crucial to recognise that if firms stop paying people in ways that broadly match their economic value and expectations, they are unlikely to successfully recruit and retain staff. On the other side of the argument, paying in excess of market norms can significantly impact on the financial performance of organisations. HR professionals have a delicate balance to achieve.

This chapter begins by focusing on the business context of reward management, considering relevant trends and factors that can impact on reward decisions. Following this section attention turns to the various ways in which reward 'intelligence' (i.e. data) can be gathered and analysed. As we analyse reward at a deeper level in the chapter, various reward perspectives, theories and principles are covered, including the concept of **'total reward'**, before specific reward incentives and practices are evaluated. Towards the end of the chapter there is a section dedicated to the role of line managers in reward management, and a final section evaluates the impact of reward management.

DEFINING REWARD MANAGEMENT

The logical place to begin this chapter is by defining the term 'reward management'. There are countless definitions available, each with a slightly different slant or approach. One of the more comprehensive definitions is from Armstrong (2007: 3), who suggests that:

> Reward management deals with the strategies, policies and processes required to ensure that the contribution of people to the organisation is recognised by both financial and non-financial means. It is about the design, implementation and maintenance of reward systems (reward processes, practices and procedures), which aim to meet the needs of both the organisation and its stakeholders. The overall objective is to reward people fairly, equitably and consistently in accordance with their value to the organisation in order to further the achievement of the organisation's strategic goals.

This definition highlights the intricacies of reward management and demonstrates that it is not solely concerned with financial issues. Armstrong (2007) specifically states that reward management involves both financial and non-financial elements, and that the overall objective of reward management is to reward people fairly, equitably and consistently.

It is notable that Armstrong suggests that reward management aims to meet the needs of both the organisation and its stakeholders. This is a point that is sometimes missed. It is important to remember that the territory of reward management is as concerned with the needs of organisational stakeholders (such as shareholders and line managers) as it is with the needs of employees. Imagine a situation in which an HR professional managed to put through a 20% pay increase for all workers at a particular company site. No doubt the employees affected would be delighted – but shareholders on the other hand might be very disappointed because their earnings from organisational profits would drop. It is crucial to recognise that HR professionals have a delicate balance to achieve in order to satisfy the many different stakeholders of reward.

THE PRINCIPLES OF REWARD MANAGEMENT

Now that the basic concept of reward management has been defined, its underlying principles must be briefly discussed before the concept as a whole can be related to the wider business environment.

As hinted at above, a key principle of reward management is that individuals in organisations are rewarded for their contributions fairly, consistently and transparently. It is important to recognise that pay itself is a very emotive issue – that is to say, that individuals can have very strong feelings about what is 'right' and what is 'wrong'. As a result of this, reward practices that are thought to be unfair can quickly break the psychological contract between employer and employee. Clear and effective communication about reward practices and decisions is therefore essential to maintain employee engagement and commitment.

A further key principle of reward management is that rewards can be either 'intrinsic' or 'extrinsic'. **Intrinsic rewards** come from work itself and can include a sense of meaningfulness, a sense of challenge and opportunities for advancement. **Extrinsic rewards** by contrast include pay, status, non-essential training and even the working environment (i.e. a more comfortable office). It is important to understand that organisations can use a combination of intrinsic and extrinsic rewards to motivate their employees, although there is no 'one best way' because the effectiveness of strategies depends to a large extent on organisational context and culture.

This introductory section of the chapter has defined the concept of reward management and introduced basic principles that underpin it. In order to arrive at a greater comprehension of where reward management 'sits' in organisations it is important to understand the business context that it operates within.

THE BUSINESS CONTEXT OF REWARD MANAGEMENT

The business context of reward management can be split into the following three broad areas:

- the international context
- the national context

- the corporate context.

This section explores these three areas before other specific contextual issues – such as those around the political environment – are examined in greater detail.

THE INTERNATIONAL CONTEXT

Global competition has demanded that organisations revise the ways in which they deliver services and products in order to produce the 'exceptional' performance that must be delivered to compete in the global marketplace. Armstrong (2002: 28) argues that the 'impact of global competition on pay systems has been to focus attention on a number of specific areas'. These include:

- flexible approaches to pay to help businesses react swiftly to new demands and pressures
- paying for performance and competence to provide competitive edge
- broad-based structures to reflect the 'lean' de-layered organisation and facilitate flexibility in the delivery of pay
- the emergence of globally mobile executives and the challenge of how they should be rewarded.

A key theme running through the list above is the need for flexibility. It is important to recognise that globalisation has an impact on the way in which organisations reward their employees, and that maintaining intransigent, outdated or inefficient models may compromise the competitiveness of firms. A further point to highlight surrounds the fact that reward management strategies and policies must be compatible with the structures of organisations. Without this link it is arguable that HR professionals will have difficulty in aligning reward management with the overall strategic goals and culture of organisations.

THE NATIONAL CONTEXT

Armstrong (2002) suggests that alongside international issues there are a number of variables at the national level that impact on reward management. For the United Kingdom these include:

- the introduction of the national minimum wage from April 1999, which affected an estimated 2 million workers
- structural change in the demand for skills. This started in the 1980s with an emphasis on high levels of attainment and expertise. Reward structures have been under pressure to adapt to encourage skill development
- structural changes in industry: a continuing shift from manufacturing to service industry, with greater complexity in associated reward practices
- fragmentation in the labour market. There are more flexible working patterns, a greater proportion of women in the labour market, a more ethnically diverse workforce, and so on. This has, for example, made it more difficult for trade unions to engage in collective bargaining, which has traditionally been applicable to blue-collar, full-time, permanent male employees in the manufacturing sector

- the lowering of inflation rates, which means that the double-digit pay awards seen in the 1970s are a thing of the past, and the view that everyone is entitled to a base pay increase each year has been challenged
- the huge gap between remuneration at the top and lower levels of the organisation, which has led to both social and legislative pressure on reward practice
- social and political trends to create new jobs in a low-inflation environment and to improve the skills of the workforce.

Perhaps the key point to draw from the list above is the structural changes that have occurred in the economy. It is vital to recognise that as the UK's economy has moved from an industrial base to a service base, reward management strategies and approaches have been adapted to fit the new context. Alongside these important changes there has also been fragmentation in the labour market. More and more individuals work part-time or have some other form of flexibility in their contractual arrangements, and this too has an impact on reward management practices. Again, reward management strategies have been adapted to take account of these changes and, as mentioned above, there is now less collective bargaining by which pay is set through negotiations between employers and trade unions.

Alongside the issues discussed above it is also important to understand that reward management in organisations is significantly influenced by politics and legislation. The following sections consider the influence that New Labour and, more recently, the Coalition Government have had on reward management practices.

New Labour

Although traditionally closely allied to the trade unions and advocates of collective bargaining, the New Labour Government elected in 1997 was reluctant to return to its 1970s policies – policies that had seen it spend nearly two decades out of power. As a result of this decision it advocated a 'third way' – one that lay between market-driven approaches and the highly interventionist approaches of previous Labour administrations. These policies contributed to the decrease in collective bargaining in organisations and encouraged public sector organisations to introduce what was called 'performance-related pay'. These pay systems included bonus elements that were tied to the achievement of specific objectives and were thought to be key ways to improve performance and increase efficiency.

The Coalition Government

During 2010 the on-going recession and presence of a large budget deficit divided electoral opinion on economic policy. The election held in 2010 reflected these divisions in that no one party was clearly re-elected. A change of government took place and a coalition was formed between the Conservatives and the Liberal Democrats. Once elected, the Coalition took action to reduce public borrowing and imposed strict cuts in government spending. In essence, the government is arguing for a much-reduced role for government and an increased role for ordinary citizens, particularly in the delivery of public services.

What implications does this shift in policy have for reward management? The government has argued for a reduction in regulation, built on its position that this constrains business and economic growth. Examples of this are the delaying of the implementation of certain provisions in the Equalities Act 2010 and the suggested extension of the qualifying period for unfair dismissal to two years. The government has committed to keeping the national minimum wage, although its level may not now increase as much annually as has hitherto been the trend.

THE CORPORATE CONTEXT

Armstrong (2002: 31) highlights the most significant aspects of the corporate environment that affect reward management:

- the impact of organisational change, particularly on corporate structures
- the impact of corporate environmental change on pay systems
- employer and employee expectations
- organisational culture
- corporate values.

Many of the factors listed above are internal to organisations but nevertheless have a substantial impact on reward. It is important to understand that these internal factors are also influenced by the external context. Employee expectations, for example, are formed within the organisation but are influenced by external variables such as education levels and comparisons that are made with family and friends who work in other organisations. Even at the corporate level, the range of influences brought to bear on reward constrains the ability of management to determine outcomes (i.e. final pay settlements, and so on) on their own terms.

REFLECTIVE ACTIVITY

In what ways does the corporate context inside your organisation (or in one with which you are familiar) shape reward management practices or systems?

Hopefully, the Reflective Activity above caused you to reflect on the specific elements of corporate culture impact on reward management. Perhaps your organisation has developed a reward system that encourages specific behaviours or attitudes. Alternatively, you may have noted that your organisation is trying to minimise costs and find efficiencies, in which case you may feel that pay systems are being tightened up or reward packages are becoming less generous overall.

CASE STUDY

Reward in the public sector

There are often substantial differences in reward practices between public and private sector organisations – not least because governments of whatever political persuasion have a role as a model employer and thus attempt to offer favourable terms and conditions of employment. This has also led to most of the public sector continuing to recognise trade unions and to collective bargaining being dominant in wage determination. We continue to see, for example, incremental pay scales, a limited emphasis on contingent pay and generous benefits in the form of flexible working, holiday entitlements and final salary pension schemes. While the *quid pro quo* for this was often argued to be lower base salaries and higher job security than the private sector, economic recession and government spending programmes have led to the erosion of salary differentials. Indeed, there have been recent claims that public sector salaries are in many instances now comparable with or superior to private sector equivalents. This has led to considerable hostility around the issue of public sector reward. Gillian Hibberd (2010), however, argues that much of this hostility is based around myths on levels of reward in the sector.

Reward in the public sector: fiction or reality?

Hibberd (2010) sets about exploding some of the myths she believes have arisen about public sector pay in recent years. She includes:

Myth 1: Public sector pensions are gold-plated. Final salary pension schemes do still exist but take-home payments from them are not, in most cases, excessive. Average salary is £13,000 and average pension £4,000.

Myth 2: The taxpayer meets the cost of all public sector pensions. There are both funded and unfunded schemes in the public sector. For example, the Local Government Scheme is funded, employer and employee contributions are invested, and pensions paid from the returns – not by the taxpayer. Employee contribution rates also vary widely – e.g. 0% for the armed forces and 11% for the police.

Myth 3: Public sector workers are paid more than their private sector equivalents. A recent Institute for Fiscal Studies (IFS) report has concluded that public sector workers are paid in line with their private sector counterparts. Raw data may not indicate this, but it needs to be adjusted to account for the often highly skilled labour that is employed in the public sector – for example, in the NHS.

Myth 4: The public sector has grown out of all control. A perception has emerged that the public sector has expanded hugely in the past decade. The IFS report suggests that public administration jobs rose by 1% and other public sector jobs by 4% in the period 2000 to 2005. These figures are now predicted to decline sharply.

Myth 5: Many public sector workers are paid more than the prime minister. Around 300 senior public sector executives earned more than the prime minister out of a workforce of over 5 million. Hibberd argues that the salaries of chief executives of public bodies are commensurate with the responsibilities they take, and less than those of most private sector senior executives.

Source: Hibberd, G. (2010) HR Column 'Fiction or reality?', *People Management*, 12 August

INTERNAL AND EXTERNAL FACTORS THAT SHAPE REWARD MANAGEMENT

Many sources, including Hatchett (2008), outline a number of pressures on reward management including inflation, rates of economic growth, labour market issues and increases in individual domestic expenditure, such as Council Tax. Alongside these issues there are a number of other factors that HR professionals need to keep in mind when setting reward strategies, including:

- the desire to maintain purchasing power: this is eroded by inflation, and workers will seek pay increases to compensate for it in order to maintain or to improve their living standards
- talent management: there has been a long period of tight labour markets in the UK, and skills shortages continue even in labour markets where there are larger numbers of unemployed individuals
- transparent pay structures: there is a greater demand both legally and socially for transparency and equity both internally and externally, and reward practices must respond to this
- equal pay issues: there have been a number of successful claims in the public sector with substantial financial implications. There is consequently a need for reward processes to support equal pay structures
- market-related comparisons: economic difficulties mean that there will be modest (or no) rises for some while others will receive higher rises in the face of skills shortages. This can create tensions within the workforce and highlights the need for transparency in pay decisions.

Alongside the issues outlined above it is important to understand that employers have a range of mechanisms for establishing job and grading systems – for example, job evaluation systems and internal labour markets – to which they attach pay structures. All of these terms are explored later in this chapter, but at the moment the key point to keep in mind is that a key justification for imposing pay and **grade structures** is to ensure that pay processes are seen to be fair.

Having said that, however, the external labour market can create problems for attempts to standardise internal systems, especially where they are applied at a national level. The price of labour in the external market may, for example, vary by geographical location. Living costs and thus wage expectations are very different in the north-east from what they are in the south-east of the UK. Similarly, there tend to be surpluses of labour in the north-east and skills shortages in the south-east. Such factors have implications for the way that pay levels are set within organisations. This discussion introduces the issue of how pay is determined in organisations. The following subsection defines the term **'pay determination'** and briefly considers how organisations go about setting pay levels in practice.

PAY DETERMINATION

'Pay determination' may appear to be a complex term at first glance but the concept is a relatively simple one. Pay determination is simply the process of making decisions about how much employees should be paid for their work. Druker and White (2009: 23) believe that:

the method and level at which decisions are taken and criteria used to determine pay levels are key issues in reward management.

This statement highlights crucial components of pay determination – the level at which decisions are made and the criteria used. Some organisations devolve pay decisions to individual managers whereas others keep control at higher levels. In the public sector, for example, salaries are often pegged against national frameworks and there is little, if any, room for manoeuvre. In the same way different organisations use different criteria to determine pay levels. In some settings skills and competencies are used as ways to set pay levels while in other environments pay may be set by reference to specific achievements against set objectives. These issues are debated in more detail a little later in this chapter.

A key external factor that impacts on the reward management decisions made by employers is legislation – notably the national minimum wage and equal pay.

THE NATIONAL MINIMUM WAGE (NMW)

The National Minimum Wage Act was passed in 1998 by the Labour Government in office at the time. It marked a shift away from a reliance on market forces to determining wages effectively, and established the first national pay rate in UK history.

From April 1999 all employers in the UK have had to pay at least the national minimum wage to their employees. Opponents of the legislation argued that an NMW would lead to higher unemployment because employers could no longer afford to employ as many staff. Opponents also suggested that inflation would increase as higher wages fed through into the economy. There is, however, very little evidence that the NMW has led to increased unemployment and inflation. Indeed, employment in traditionally low-wage sectors such as hospitality and retail has continued to grow since the introduction of the NMW.

In April 1999 the NMW was set at £3.60 per hour (£3.00 for 18- to 21-year-olds). By 2011 the headline rate had increased to £6.08 per hour for individuals aged 21 or more, although there were separate rates for those aged 18 to 20 (£4.98 per hour) and those aged between 16 and 17 (£3.68 per hour).

Alongside the introduction of the NMW employers also have to contend with equal pay legislation.

EQUAL PAY

There are several pieces of legislation that impact on reward decisions, including those around equal pay and discrimination. The Equal Pay Act 1970 (as amended by the Equal Pay (Amendment) Regulations 1983) now incorporated into the Equality Act 2010 was needed to address pay discrimination on the grounds of gender. For example, as noted by Perkins and White (2011: 77), until the passing of the Equal Pay Act in 1970 it was perfectly legal to pay women less than men for doing the same job. Legislation now prevents this from occurring.

Equal pay legislation defines pay as wages and all other contractual entitlements, including holiday and sick pay, for example, as well as any discounts offered by the employer and 'benefits in kind'. The specific provisions of the legislation around equal pay now provide for the right for men and women to be paid the same in the following three circumstances:

- for like work (where two employees are doing exactly the same or very similar work)
- for work rated as equivalent (how this rating should be arrived at is not specified in law but is often informed by **job evaluation**)
- for work of equal value (where jobs are very different in terms of their skills and abilities but contribute a similar amount of 'value' to the organisation).

 Equal pay, or more-than-equal pay?

CASE STUDY

Gemma Cartwright and Steven Garth work in the same organisation doing work of equal value. At present she earns £20,000 and Steven earns £21,000. A job evaluation exercise is conducted, but the results are not communicated because they are considered too politically sensitive. No changes are made to salaries. Gemma learns via the organisational grapevine that her post was evaluated 25% above

Steven's. She takes the organisation to an employment tribunal and wins her case. What should her new salary be?

- £25,000?
- £26,000?

or

- £21,000?

GATHERING AND ANALYSING REWARD INTELLIGENCE

There are many sources of reward management data that HR practitioners can take advantage of. The CIPD, for instance, produces an annual reward management survey, which examines issues such as pay positioning, pensions and benefits and performance-related bonuses. Alongside reports produced by professional institutions such as the CIPD there are also various industry benchmarking reports and surveys, including those produced by the local government group for the public sector and private sector organisations such as Croner (www.croner.co.uk) and Incomes Data Services (www.incomesdata.co.uk).

Together with the data sources listed above, national statistics also have relevance within reward management. Before making pay decisions HR professionals often need to take account of the following factors:

- inflation
- unemployment rates
- the number of vacancies
- average working hours

• average earnings.

Information relating to factors such as inflation, unemployment rates and average earnings/working hours can be found from government websites such as www.statistics.gov.uk. By examining these sorts of data sources HR professionals can quickly identify trends in particular areas and can adapt their reward management strategies and decisions as a result. When thinking about the number of vacancies, it is important to recognise that positions that are particularly difficult to fill generally command higher reward packages. Vacancies that attract many applicants, by contrast, can usually be given lower reward packages – although this is not always the case.

When examining reward management data it is important to recognise that statistics can be influenced by issues occurring at a variety of different levels. The previous section of this chapter considered the international, national and corporate contexts of reward management, and it is important to understand that these factors shape the ways in which organisations make their final decisions. Alongside these considerations, as we saw above, HR professionals must also take the effect of legislation into account when gathering and analysing reward data.

Before moving on to examine the various theories of reward management, it is important to consider the ways in which reward data may be presented to various stakeholder groups. The primary consideration here is the level and type of data that is going to be relevant to each group. Whereas senior managers might want to see detailed benchmarking data from comparable organisations or data that allows them to gauge how factors such as inflation or the number of vacancies are affecting reward management, other stakeholders may have different requirements. Employees, for example, are unlikely to be concerned with specific comparisons between particular roles but they are likely to want to know how their earnings compare to the average across an industry. It is important that HR professionals can provide appropriate information for each specific stakeholder group.

From the discussions in this section it should be clear that there are a variety of internal and external factors that influence reward management in organisations. To add greater complexity to the lives of HR practitioners there are also several underpinning theories that inform the reward management field. These theories shed more light on reward management decisions. However, their positions frequently contradict. It is important to understand that there is not necessarily one theory that is 'right' or one theory that is 'wrong' – they are simply different interpretations that may or may not be relevant in given contexts.

THEORIES OF REWARD MANAGEMENT

It is important to understand that there are a variety of perspectives and theories that exist within the reward management field. This part of the chapter outlines and discusses the main theories and perspectives:

• economic theory
• institutional theories of reward

● human capital theory.

Please do not be put off by the terminology in the bullet list above. The theories are relatively straightforward and the key principles of each are explained in detail.

ECONOMIC THEORY

Economic theories broadly consider wage rates to be determined by a combination of the supply of labour and the demand for that labour from employers. Wage rates are therefore arrived at to try to achieve a balance between supply and demand. If labour is in short supply, the value of the labour increases and wages go up. Conversely, where labour is plentiful, its value drops. Key assumptions of economic theories are firstly that both employers and employees are rational actors who have all the information they need to make informed choices, and secondly that employees are fully mobile – that is, they will move to where there are jobs available.

There are, however, complexities within these theories. Firstly, of course, not many employees are really 'fully mobile' because they are constrained by family and social circumstances. So the opportunity to maximise their reward is limited. Secondly, economic theories focus only on forms of financial reward to attract labour and achieve organisational goals. Within these theories the 'worth' of the potential employee and the state of the labour market are the features that determine wage rates. A criticism of these assumptions has been provided by individuals who are more disposed towards what are termed social psychological theories. Social psychologists emphasise, instead, the long-term nature of the employment relationship and suggest that economic theories that focus only on pay rates do not accurately reflect reality. They suggest that it is more important for employees to experience job satisfaction and a sense of fairness in relation to reward. It is important to understand that tensions in the employment relationship can lead to the adoption of different perspectives on reward.

INSTITUTIONAL THEORIES OF REWARD

Perhaps unsurprisingly, given all the above criticism of economic theories, there are a number of other economic theories that seek to explain how wage rates are established. These have all influenced thinking in different ways, rather than one being superior to or replacing another theory. This is an important point to keep in mind.

Institutional theories of reward introduce a more 'open systems' approach to setting wage levels. They recognise the role of institutions within reward systems – in other words, context or environmental factors are recognised as influencing wage levels. An open systems approach allows for the possibility of an employer's actions in the use of wages to influence employee attitudes and behaviours. An example of an employer action might be if an employer offered a wage premium in order to attract labour. Such a decision might motivate workers to focus their efforts on achieving organisational strategy. In addition to this point it is important to remember that workers do not necessarily 'sell' their labour as individuals: they may act collectively (most obviously through a trade union) and such activity will affect wages. The sizes of organisations or of industry sectors are also thought to influence pay-setting.

Institutional theorists argue that recognition of these factors helps to explain why wage levels rarely appear to fall. Classical economic labour market theories such as those explored above suggest that wages will be lower when there is a surplus of labour, but in reality wages are often described as 'sticky' – that is, they are resistant to being reduced. It can certainly be argued that trade union activity may well achieve this outcome, because workers operating collectively often prevent any reduction in their pay. There are a number of competing explanations for the 'stickiness' of wages, and it is important to understand that this issue is not generally well understood.

HUMAN CAPITAL THEORY

Human capital theory (Becker, 1975) is one of the founding theories in understanding reward. This theory suggests that workers 'invest' in themselves via education, training and development to increase their own capital (or value to employers). Different levels of reward are used to attract workers dependent upon their skills, experience and qualifications. In other words, the higher an individual's capital, the higher is the return on it in terms of pay and benefits as organisations compete for skilled labour.

REFLECTIVE ACTIVITY

Which of the theoretical approaches outlined here do you think best fits with the reward management practices and systems inside your organisation (or one that you know well)?

THE CONCEPT OF 'TOTAL REWARD'

The term 'total reward' is often used in modern reward management systems, but what does it actually mean? The CIPD (2009) states that total reward is:

> the term that has been adopted to describe a reward strategy that brings additional components such as learning and development, together with aspects of the working environment, into the benefits package. It goes beyond standard remuneration by embracing the company culture, and is aimed at giving all employees a voice in the operation, with the employer in return receiving an engaged employee performance.

This definition demonstrates that total reward considers far more than just base pay and that it 'embraces the company culture'. It highlights the holistic nature of total reward, and this is a key point to keep in mind. Within this interpretation the basic elements of a total reward package include:

- financial compensation
- benefits

- work–life balance
- performance and recognition
- development and career opportunities.

The key learning point in this section, then, is that a total reward approach involves both extrinsic and intrinsic elements. An example in practice can be seen in the case study below, which has been taken from *People Management*.

Charities use total reward to make work staff's own Eden

CASE STUDY

Third-sector organisations can achieve success with a total reward approach to make up for their inability to offer high salaries, delegates at this month's CIPD Reward Forum heard.

Leah Brewer, organisational development manager at the Eden Trust, explained how the environmental charity had pioneered a range of innovative benefits, including on-site yoga, podiatry and massages. High-performing employees are nominated for one-off bonuses, vouchers for the Eden Project shop, or a one-to-one lunch with Tim Smit, Eden's chief executive. Workers are also entered into a draw to take an extra week's annual leave.

'Working for Eden is rewarding, and not only for the pay packet,' said Brewer. 'It's important to make sure it works for the organisation as well as the individual.'

Firms should not be afraid to try new things when it comes to reward, and while pilot schemes are a good way of getting management buy-in, not everything will work, she said.

'Sometimes knock-backs can be good – you have a reason why [a scheme didn't work] and you can deal with that,' Brewer told *PM*.

Joe Bennett, HR director at Scope, told delegates that performance-related pay had proved a success at the charity, although it concentrated on senior staff.

'HR can add value by focusing its attention on that particular group of people and really getting them to excel,' said Bennett. 'To help get a feeling of clarity and consistency, you have to get the messages right. You need the top team banging out those messages.'

Source: Chubb, L. (2007) 'Charities use total reward to make work staff's own Eden', *People Management*, 29 November.

REFLECTIVE ACTIVITY

Does your organisation (or one that you used to work in) use a 'total reward' approach? Do you think that this has/would have any effect on your level of engagement with your organisation?

THE AIMS OF TOTAL REWARD

Although there are many different models of total reward that organisations can adopt, the CIPD states that 'the principle of viewing a range of non-financial factors as part of the rewards package' is the same. Many organisations are now looking at the experience they offer in a more holistic manner when deciding how best to attract, retain and engage existing and potential employees. The broad aim of a total reward approach is to achieve a better balance between the needs of the employee and the needs of the organisation.

Looking at the fundamental purpose of total reward a little more closely, Armstrong (2007: 31) believes that the central aim is 'to maximise the combined impact of a wide range of reward initiatives on motivation, commitment and job engagement'. There is a broad view that total reward should aim to increase employee satisfaction and ultimately business performance. To this end the CIPD (2009) maintains that the aim of total reward should be to obtain 'more positive employee commitment without incurring open-ended operational costs'. This statement confirms the view that total reward aims to balance the needs of the employee with the needs of the employer. Having now understood the broad aim of total reward, let us consider its benefits in an organisational setting.

THE BENEFITS OF TOTAL REWARD

The CIPD Factsheet on Total Reward (2009) states that there are four key benefits of such strategies. These are thought to be:

- the easier recruitment of talented staff
- reduced wastage through staff turnover
- better business performance
- the enhanced reputation of the organisation as an employer of choice.

Whereas these points may seem appropriate from a theoretical stance, how might they translate to operational practice? Empirical evidence gathered from Buckinghamshire County Council, where total reward was introduced in 2006, displays evidence of the benefits listed above being realised in practice (Hibberd, 2009). The results from this particular study included the following findings:

- Confidence in the leadership of the authority rose by 21%.
- 80% of staff felt 'well recognised' for the work they did (an increase of 3%).
- Those who felt 'valued' increased by 7%.
- 91% of employees enjoyed being part of a team (a rise of 13%).
- 76% of staff enjoyed working for the Council.

Hibberd (2009) believes that total reward sends a strong message to the workforce. The findings above arguably demonstrate that the organisation in question is perceived to *care* about its employees, which is an important factor when using reward to foster engagement. Hibberd (2009) suggested at a later conference that the public sector needed to communicate the value of total reward in a more effective way in order to retain top talent. Hibberd pointed out that if this could not be done, talented members of staff might be tempted to move to the private sector once it emerges from recession and starts to create large numbers of jobs once again.

REWARD INITIATIVES AND PRACTICES

The focus of this part of the chapter is on specific reward initiatives and practices. In broad terms this territory incorporates:

- grade and pay structures
- job evaluation
- market rate analysis
- 'contingent' reward.

Please do not be put off by the terminology above. The text explains and discusses the concepts in detail in order to convey a detailed understanding of reward initiatives and practices.

GRADE AND PAY STRUCTURES

Grade and pay structures are important parts of reward management. When they are designed properly and fit effectively within the wider context of the organisation, they provide a logical framework within which an organisation's pay policies can be implemented. Grade and pay structures help HR professionals work out where jobs should be placed in a hierarchy, define appropriate pay levels, and demonstrate how pay can be progressed over time.

In simple terms, a grade structure is made up of a number of grades, bands or levels into which groups of comparable jobs can be placed. Organisations may choose to operate a single-grade structure into which all jobs are placed, or they may choose to group jobs into job or career 'families'. Either approach can be appropriate: suitability is determined by contextual variables such as the size and complexity of the organisation.

Along similar lines to the thoughts outlined above, a pay structure defines the different levels of pay for jobs or groups of jobs by reference to their relative value to the organisation. Relative value can be determined in a number of ways including job evaluation and market rate analysis (both of these concepts are discussed shortly). As with grade structures, an organisation may decide to implement one pay structure for all employees or it may choose to operate different structures within different occupational groups. Armstrong (2006) points out that organisations are increasingly looking to harmonise terms and conditions of employment, so that single pay structures are becoming more and more common.

Broadly, there are several different types of grade and pay structures that organisations may choose to operate. The most common are:

- narrow-graded
- broad-graded
- job family
- career family

- pay spines.

As you may imagine, narrow-graded structures have many different pay and grade levels (more than 10 and sometimes as many as 18) whereas broad-graded structures have fewer levels. It is important to understand that within broad-graded structures there may be reference points placed within each grade or level, perhaps splitting each into two or three segments.

By contrast to the approaches above, job family structures seek to group jobs functionally or operationally – in other words, splitting the IT roles from the finance roles or production roles from research roles. Along similar lines, career family structures seek to split roles into different career paths but try to ensure comparability between different families. In other words a 'junior' finance role is pegged at the same level as a 'junior' administration role, and so on.

Armstrong (2006) tells us that pay spines are often found in the public sector and in organisations that have adopted a public sector approach to reward management. These systems consist of a number of different pay 'points' extending from the lowest- to the highest-paid positions in an organisation. Increments can be placed at regular intervals – perhaps 2% or 3% of salary – or organisations may choose to widen the gaps between jobs towards the top of the hierarchy. It is very important to understand that there is no 'one best way' to set up a grade or pay structure. An approach that may be appropriate in one organisation may be unworkable in another, and *vice versa*.

JOB EVALUATION

At its most simple, a job evaluation scheme is a systematic process for defining the relative worth or size of jobs within an organisation. The main reason why HR professionals undertake job evaluations is to assess which jobs in an organisation are similar in order to plot their position within grade or pay structures. Job evaluation schemes aim to:

- establish where jobs in an organisation are of similar size or value
- allow for the development of equitable and defendable pay and grade structures
- help practitioners make market comparisons about specific roles
- provide internal transparency for all stakeholders
- ensure that organisations meet equal pay obligations.

Broadly, job evaluation schemes can be either 'analytical' or 'non-analytical'. Analytical job evaluation is by far the more common approach and revolves around analysing specific factors such as competencies and making objective decisions about the relative value of specific roles. Whereas analytical job evaluation seeks to compare and contrast different factors within roles, non-analytical job evaluation seeks to compare whole jobs and place them into a grade or rank order. It is important to understand that non-analytical job evaluation schemes do not meet the requirements of equal value legislation although they can still be useful exercises to broadly assess jobs within an organisation.

Although job evaluation can be a useful method of comparing jobs internally, it is not suitable for making comparisons between organisations. In order to make comparisons of jobs or grades between organisations, a process known as market rate analysis must be used.

MARKET RATE ANALYSIS

It is very important to understand that pay levels within organisations are subject to external as well as internal pressures. Whereas job evaluation schemes can be used to determine internal relativities, HR professionals can only determine external relativities by using a technique called market rate analysis.

Armstrong (2006) points out that the concept of the market rate is an imprecise one. He argues that there is no such thing as *the* market rate, and that there are a variety of rates paid by employers even where jobs appear to be identical. Organisations do this for a number of reasons – perhaps a skill shortage in a particular geographical location has pushed up the salary for a particular position, or maybe an organisation has adopted a cost-minimisation model and consequently pays below the market average.

In order to conduct a market rate analysis HR professionals must gather and analyse data related to the salaries and reward packages offered by similar organisations. It is very important to understand that data can often be misleading or incomplete, and HR professionals have to be very careful to make accurate comparisons. When making market comparisons the aim should be to:

- acquire accurate data that correctly details base pay, bonuses and benefits, as was analysed above
- compare like with like – in other words, compare rewards attached to jobs of similar size and importance
- ensure that collected information is up to date
- interpret the information with an eye on the organisation's current needs and circumstances
- collate and present the information in such a way that actions become clear.

CONTINGENT REWARD

At first glance the concept of **contingent reward** looks confusing, but it is essentially focused around two basic questions: what do we value, and what are we prepared to pay for? Armstrong (2006) points out that there are many different contingent reward strategies that firms can adopt, including performance-related pay, competence-related pay, skill-based pay and team-based pay. All of these approaches link pay to some form of variable (such as job performance or personal competence), but organisations can take different approaches to the structure of their reward offering.

Most firms that operate some form of contingent reward strategy provide employees with an element of base pay and a bonus related to whatever factor they deem to be important. Within performance-related pay systems this might be individual performance against a set of objectives, whereas within skill-based pay a bonus might be linked to the acquisition of new skills. There are many terms for this bonus element, including 'variable' pay or 'pay at risk'.

Contingent pay systems are popular in organisations because many individuals see them as the best way to motivate people. They assume that linking an element of pay to the achievement of a particular goal will encourage employees to achieve that goal. Having considered the topic of total reward at an earlier point of this chapter, it can be argued that this view of contingent pay is perhaps a little simplistic. Within total reward systems individuals are thought to be motivated by intrinsic factors as well as extrinsic factors. It is important to remember that pay itself is an extrinsic motivator whereas the satisfaction derived from work can often be an intrinsic motivator. HR professionals must ensure that they strike the right balance between extrinsic and intrinsic motivators in their policy frameworks.

REFLECTIVE ACTIVITY

What benefits might contingent reward offer organisations? Do you think the use of contingent reward improves organisational performance?

The Reflective Activity above should have made you think about the applicability of contingent reward. In broad terms it may be argued that contingent reward systems can help to support improved organisational performance because they focus individuals on certain activities and can be used to highlight particularly important goals or targets. But you may think that they are potentially divisive and too subjective in their measurement. Both would be partly true. The use of contingent pay has to be carefully managed and fit with the organisation's goal and culture. Below is a case study that illustrates how an organisation made changes to its contingent reward scheme on the basis that the scheme did not match its strategy.

Nationwide

Nationwide Building Society operates over 700 branches, within which there are around 450 senior financial consultants (SFCs). They sell many products that are regulated by the Financial Services Authority. The pay and bonus scheme for SFCs required an overhaul for several reasons: it focused on volume rather than value; it was not cost-effective; and it didn't differentiate sufficiently between low and high performance. Because any changes to the reward schemes were contractual, they required full union negotiation. As a result a new total reward package

that met all the outlined criteria was launched four months after the project was started in January 2009. Following a comprehensive communication programme asking SFCs how they should be rewarded, the reward team gained full union support. Staff feedback was also positive. Sales performance in the quarter following launch increased to 184% of target.

Source: *People Management* (2010) 'CIPD People Management Awards

2010: Performance and reward
category', 12 August.

LINE MANAGERS AND REWARD MANAGEMENT

As with many areas of HR practice, line managers play an important role in reward management systems and processes. Line managers are the individuals who have most contact with employees and are normally responsible for making pay decisions within the frameworks set out by HR professionals. For this reason line managers have a crucial dimension in maintaining fairness, consistency and transparency across organisations. It is important to understand that these individuals need to be trained in how reward systems work and how decisions should be arrived at.

Towards the beginning of this chapter the fact that reward management consists of both extrinsic factors (such as pay and benefits) and intrinsic factors (such as work itself being meaningful) was highlighted. Line managers have a crucial role to play in enhancing intrinsic rewards and can do it by designing jobs so that employees can feel a sense of purpose at work and by providing praise as and when necessary. Reward management does not revolve solely around monetary pay and benefits, as was shown earlier in this chapter when the concept of total reward was investigated.

Despite the points outlined above, line managers often do not feel involved in reward management – and this can consequently affect employee commitment and engagement. HR professionals must take time to ensure that line managers are consulted about reward management decisions and must make sure that their views are taken into consideration. HR professionals must explain grade and pay structures to line managers and indicate where and when rewards, whether financial or non-financial, might be distributed. If organisations operate some form of contingent pay system, line managers are a vital source of information regarding performance, competence and/or employee skill. Again, it is vital that HR practitioners provide line managers with the necessary training so that they can make objective judgements about relative levels of performance, competence and/or skill – otherwise, final reward decisions may not be consistent or even fair.

Throughout this chapter it has been shown that reward management is an area of practice that is deeply affected by both external and internal variables, including the business context as a whole, legislative decisions and organisational strategies. If line managers are not supported in making effective reward decisions, reward systems and processes will be redundant. No matter how much thought has gone into grade or pay structures, if line managers do not know how they apply in practical ways, there will be no consistency of reward across the organisation.

EVALUATING THE IMPACT OF REWARD MANAGEMENT

Organisations must take time to assess the impact of reward management to ensure that strategic decisions are having the desired effect. Evaluation is often an overlooked area but it is important to understand that it need not be a laborious process.

In previous sections it was noted that HR professionals might benchmark their reward strategies or packages against those of their competitors. Although this might be an easier task in public sector environments where information is perhaps more freely available, there are surveys such as those conducted by the CIPD that HR professionals might find useful. By analysing organisational performance against these benchmarks broad trends can be found and reported back to senior managers. In addition to external benchmarks HR professionals can also make use of tools such as staff surveys to attempt to spot any correlations between reward management and both employee commitment and engagement. By examining trends over several surveys HR professionals may be able to highlight the impacts of certain decisions and policies, and produce convincing evidence to support their business cases or proposals.

In addition to the measures outlined above, it is quite possible that HR professionals will be able to link employee performance with reward decisions. By taking time to analyse data emerging from staff appraisals or performance management processes, HR professionals will be able to indicate where specific reward practices are having an impact. Perhaps a team-based bonus might be found to be contributing to more effective teamworking in a particular department, or perhaps a higher starting salary in another department might have attracted a more skilled workforce. Of course, findings always differ between organisations, but if accurate data is collected, HR professionals should be able to make a judgement about the effectiveness of reward strategies and policies.

 Merit based pay versus yearly rises for all

CASE STUDY

Please take some time to carefully read through the article from *People Management* presented below, which discusses the idea that organisations prefer 'merit-based' pay increases as opposed to yearly rises for everyone. Once you are happy that you understand the key points from the article, see if you can answer the three questions that appear at the end.

Firms prefer merit-based pay to yearly rises for all

Almost half (46%) of organisations no longer award employees an across-the-board annual rise or cost-of-living adjustment, the Reward Management 2008 survey has revealed. Manufacturing, production and private sector firms were the least likely to provide such a pay rise. An increasingly popular alternative is to allocate pay budgets to departmental heads to distribute among staff based on their contribution, the survey of 603 organisations found. 'The decline in the yearly traditional pay rise seems to be spreading throughout employment sectors,' said Charles Cotton, CIPD adviser, reward and employment conditions. [...]

David Conroy, principal of the human capital business at HR consultancy Mercer, said that 20% of pay deals now have a long-term nature. While this helps employers by making planning more predictable, sweeteners are often needed to overcome union reservations, said Conroy. 'Sometimes there are other benefits bundled in as a way of encouraging the workforce to agree to a deal, such as improvements to annual leave and to maternity and paternity provision,' he said.

Cotton warned that any changes to pay and benefits needed to be effectively communicated by line managers to their teams to avoid leaving staff 'confused, demotivated and in the dark about what they need to do to achieve reward and recognition'.

Paul Ryan, HR operations manager at consumer brands firm Henkel, told PM that across-the-board pay increases in the private sector run counter to the principle of basing rises on merit.

'High-potential staff won't find it motivating if they are told their pay will progress at a mediocre rate whatever they do,' he said. Ryan, who is responsible for compensation and benefits for the company's 1,150 UK staff, added that most people in the private sector were 'conditioned to be more flexible' but admitted that multi-year pay deals might be more commonplace in highly unionised environments.

Meanwhile, unions in the public sector have expressed concern that the government's new longer-term pay deals, which will initially focus on teachers, nurses and the police, may amount to pay cuts in real terms. They have demanded 'escape clauses' if economic conditions change during the three-year period.

Source: Phillips, L. (2008) 'Firms prefer merit-based pay to yearly rises for all', *People Management*, 24 January.

Questions

1   Why might firms prefer merit-based pay increases rather than standard annual pay rises for all?

2   Evaluate the role that line managers play in communicating pay decisions to employees. Why are they such important individuals in this process?

3   In what ways might the external context facing organisations influence decisions related to pay increases?

FURTHER READING

Armstrong, M. (2010) *A Handbook of Reward Management Practice*, 3rd edition. London, Kogan Page. This is a useful resource, which covers both theory and best practice in the reward management field.

Churchard, C. (2010) 'Reward professionals go "back to the drawing board"', *People Management*, 23 February. This *People Management* article discusses reward strategies and priorities in the wake of the recent recession.

Churchard, C. (2011) 'Creative non-cash rewards "drive key staff behaviours"', *People Management*, 1 November. This *People Management* article discusses how employers might be able to get more value for their money by investing in 'non-cash' rewards.

CIPD (2012) *Reward Management* Information Page. [Online] Available at: http://www.cipd.co.uk/hr-topics/reward-management.aspx. This website provides factsheets, podcasts and survey reports on the subject of reward management.

E-Reward (2012) *E-Reward: The online guide to reward management.* [Online] Available at: http://www.e-reward.co.uk/. This website provides practical guidance, 'top tips' and links to other websites which contain reward management content.

Hall, J. (2012) 'Hundreds of gold-plated final salary pension schemes close', *The Daily Telegraph*, 31 January. This article discusses the move from final salary to 'defined contribution' pension schemes.

Perkins, S. and White, G. (2011) *Reward Management*, 2nd edition. London, Chartered Institute of Personnel and Development. This CIPD text discusses the overall context of reward management, explores key conceptual frameworks and discusses the various elements of pay- and benefit-setting in detail.

REFERENCES

Armstrong, M. (2002) *Employee Reward*. London, Chartered Institute of Personnel and Development.

Armstrong, M. (2006) *A Handbook of Human Resource Management Practice*, 10th edition. London, Kogan Page.

Armstrong, M. (2007) *A Handbook of Reward Management Practice*, 2nd edition. London, Kogan Page.

Becker, G. (1975) *Human Capital: A theoretical and empirical analysis, with special reference to education*, 2nd edition. Chicago, University of Chicago Press.

CIPD (2009) *Total Reward*. Factsheet. June. London, Chartered Institute of Personnel and Development.

Croner (2012) Croner. [Online] Available at: www.croner.co.uk [accessed 11 February 2012].

Druker, J. and White, G. (2009) *Reward Management: A critical text*, 2nd edition. London, Routledge.

Hatchett, A. (2008) 'Area of high pressure as cold front approaches', *People Management*, 10 January.

Hibberd, G. (2009) 'Engage staff through total reward', *Employee Benefits*, 16 January.

Hibberd, G. (2010) 'Fiction or reality?', HR Column, *People Management*, 12 August.

IDS (2012) *IDS: Employment Information and Analysis*. [Online] Available at: www.incomesdata.co.uk [accessed 11 February 2012].

Office for National Statistics (2012) UK National Statistics: Publication Hub. [Online] Available at: www.statistics.gov.uk [accessed 12 February 2012].

Perkins, S. J. and White, G. (2011) *Reward Management*, 2nd edition. London, Chartered Institute of Personnel and Development.

Phillips, L. (2008) 'Firms prefer merit-based pay to yearly rises for all', *People Management*, 24 January.

Glossary

Benchmarking The comparison between one organisation and another of an internal process, system or method in terms of its efficiency, effectiveness and/or cost.

Claimant A person who, using a claim form, brings a case against an organisation before an employment tribunal.

Common law Law created as a precedent by a judge in a court rather than by Act of Parliament. The common law evolves as cases are brought before the courts (and if necessary through progressively higher courts). Court decisions and rulings then become binding precedents that lower courts must always follow.

Competency framework A written set of attributes or competencies that an organisation is looking for in staff who work in particular jobs. In many cases, but not all, such frameworks are derived from a systematic study of the characteristics of top performers in those jobs within the organisation.

Constructive dismissal A situation in which an employee resigns as a direct result of an actual or anticipated breach of contract on the part of his or her employer. If the breach is proven, the courts may award remedial compensation to the 'dismissed' employee.

Contingent reward Pay based not on any established scale or measure but on what an organisation most values at the time and is prepared (and able) to pay for.

Contract of employment A legally binding agreement made between an employer and employee detailing specific facts about a specific job, the written and implied terms of which are enforceable in the courts.

Employee engagement The positive emotional input with which employees are committed to an organisation and to their work, and willing to work hard to achieve objectives. Prime indicators are good communication systems and evidence of partnership working.

Employee involvement A form of employee voice intended to elicit ideas and input from employees. Examples include upward and downward communication, and problem-solving groups.

Employee participation A form of employee voice intended to share power between management and employees. Examples include joint consultation committees and works councils.

Employer branding A 'set of attributes and qualities, often intangible, that makes an organisation distinctive, promises a particular kind of employment experience, and appeals to those people who will thrive and perform best in its culture'.

Employment tribunals Courts which have statutory jurisdiction in handling employment-related matters and which are presided over by employment judges.

The Employment Appeal Tribunal (EAT) The first court of appeal to which appeals from employment tribunals are taken by parties who wish to contest a ruling on a point of law.

European Court of Justice The European Union's high court based in Luxembourg: the final court of appeal for cases that relate to European law.

Extrinsic reward Reward expected following the completion of work. Examples of extrinsic rewards include pay and status.

Grade/pay structure A collection of pay grades, levels or bands linking related jobs within a hierarchy or series, that provides a framework for the implementation of reward strategies and policies within an organisation.

Gross misconduct A breach of an employer's rules that is so serious as to justify summary dismissal (being sacked on the spot) without notice.

High-performance working (HPW) Superior, sustained high performance achieved by employees in an organisation, linked to a bundle of sophisticated employee-centred HR practices.

Industrial action Sustained measure (in the form of activity or inactivity) taken by a group of workers – usually organised by a trade union – aimed at securing concessions from an employer. Strikes are the most common form.

Insight-driven Guided by the power (generally on the part of management) to discern and understand, involving imagination, practical knowledge and enlightenment.

Intrinsic reward Reward that comes from and is inherent in the work itself. Examples of intrinsic rewards include a sense of accomplishment and opportunities for advancement.

Involuntary turnover The proportion of the total number of employments that come to an end, which were terminated at the behest of the employer.

Job evaluation A systematic process for defining the relative worth or size of jobs within an organisation.

Labour market The pool of potential workers available to an organisation – they might be local, national or global.

Labour turnover The rate at which employees leave an organisation, usually expressed as a proportional percentage. A labour turnover rate of 10% means that one in every 10 employees leaves per year (either voluntarily or involuntarily).

Loose labour market A labour market in which there are a large number of individuals looking for employment, and job vacancies are in relatively short supply.

Management style The ways in which managers use their power and authority in the workplace. Examples are listed in Purcell and Sisson's (1983) typology of management style.

Mediation A process for resolving conflict in the workplace involving a third party, which aims to find a resolution that is acceptable to both parties involved in a dispute.

Menus of intervention Schedules of useful positive actions intended to be taken.

Organisational change Ways and processes in which an organisation moves from where it is now towards where it wants to be. This may involve changes to its structures, systems and culture, which may in turn alter the nature, shape and skill sets of its workforce.

Pay determination The complex process of calculating and deciding on how much employees should be paid for their work.

Pluralist Describing the view that conflict is an inevitable feature of employment relationships owing to the different (plural) interests of managers and of employees/trade unions. Following the theory derived from the work of Fox (1966) relating to the ways in which managers view employment relationships, pluralists emphasise the need for the management of conflict at work.

Psychological contract The employment relationship regarded primarily as an exchange of obligations and understood commitments between employer and employee.

Recruitment Methods by which potentially suitable employees are sought – including advertising and head-hunting – located, and eventually introduced to an organisation.

Redundancy Termination of employment because there has been, or is going to be, a collapse of the business, a closure of the workplace, or a diminution in the need for employees.

Retirement Termination of his or her employment by an individual who has decided to leave the labour market because of advancing age. There is no longer a default retirement age, so that the timing of retirement is now largely a matter of employee choice.

Reward management The operation of strategies, policies and processes required to ensure that the contribution of people to an organisation is appropriately recognised by both financial and non-financial means.

Selection Methods by which the most suitable individual for a job vacancy is chosen from the pool of individuals who have applied.

Self-service technologies The means by which managers are able to directly access technology-driven HR assistance, enabling them to carry out a range of HR activities independently.

Stability Measure of the length of time employees in general remain with an organisation (more properly known as the stability index). It is commonly used in conjunction with staff turnover.

Staff turnover The proportion of employees who leave the organisation over any specified period of time, expressed as a percentage of the total number of staff employed. It is commonly used in conjunction with stability.

Statutes Laws that are passed by Parliament and that are enforced in the courts. Statutes take the form either of Acts of Parliament or of Regulations issued by Ministers under the terms of individual Acts.

Structural transformation The process in which the structure of an organisation is reorganised to reflect the changing demands placed upon it.

Supreme Court Formerly the House of Lords, the highest court to which appeals can be made in the UK's judicial system. Only if a matter concerns European Law is a further appeal possible.

Tight labour market A labour market in which there are a large number of employers looking for workers with certain skills, and these workers are in relatively short supply.

Total reward A strategy that incorporates additional components such as learning and development, together with progressive aspects of the working environment, within the overall reward/benefits package.

Trade union An organisation independent from employing organisations that represents the individual and collective interests of its members in relation to the terms and conditions of employment.

Transactional Describing the day-to-day business conducted within existing arrangements and processes. In HR terms this would include payroll and pensions, legal services, recruitment and selection, employee assistance and training.

Transformational Describing activity centred on changes to the structure, processes, systems and ways of working to better reflect changing demands and pressures.

Unitarist Describing the view that the relationship between employers and employees is basically harmonious (unitary) and co-operative, united behind the authority of the manager in pursuit of the organisation's goals. It is an alternative perspective to the pluralist view.

Voluntary turnover The proportion of the total number of employments that come to an end, which were terminated by the choice of individual employees.

Index

Student resources

Your dedicated online area giving you all you need, when you need it. Helpful factsheets to guide you in revision and preparing for exams, practical tools, online journals and much more can be found at **cipd.co.uk/studyresources**

Students can **save 20%** on textbooks

Plus **save 10%** on CIPD training, online subscription products, conference tickets, publications, DVDs and Toolkits.

To find out more, call us on +44 (0)20 8612 6208 or visit cipd.co.uk/memberbenefits